RELATIONSHIP WEALTH

RELATIONSHIP WEALTH

THE ESSENTIAL NEEDS THAT PREDICT
RELATIONSHIP SUCCESS - AND HOW TO SATISFY
THEM

J. LARRY CALDWELL

VICTORIA CROWN PUBLICATIONS

ISBN 978-0-9886400-3-0 (Paperback)

ISBN 978-0-9886400-4-7 (Hard cover)

ISBN 978-0-9886400-5-4 (eBook)

First Edition

Published by Victoria Crown Publications

Printed in the United States of America

CONTENTS

INTRODUCTION

A lifelong dream for most people is to lead a rich and meaningful life. When asked to define a quality life, most will emphasize the importance of having successful, lasting relationships. Our natural desire to seek positive and satisfying connections with others is a fundamental part of being human. The desire for close relationships is universal—transcending nationalities, races, and culture.

Quality relationships offer profound benefits that add meaning to one's life. These benefits include a sense of belonging and support, increased life satisfaction, better psychological and physical health, and a deeper sense of purpose.

While most people want to have a quality intimate relationship, many will find this to be an elusive dream that often feels out of reach. While the desire for intimacy is strong, numerous individuals find themselves unable to achieve or sustain a fulfilling partnership.

Relationships often falter when faced with life's inevitable challenges—not because of a lack of love, but because partners often lack the skills or understanding needed to effectively navigate those challenges.

This lack of ability can take many forms. Some partners find it difficult to express love in ways that meet their partner's needs, while others face deeper conflicts rooted in incompatible values and priorities. In truth, all relationships involve some degree of incompatibility —what matters most is how couples respond and adapt to those differences.

While the benefits of quality relationships are well documented, the costs of relationship failure are often underestimated. Distressed or broken relationships can result in profound emotional costs, not only for the individuals involved, but also for their families, and especially their children. The fallout often includes significant feelings of depression, loneliness, anxiety, and insecurity, all of which can have a serious, long-lasting impact on emotional well-being and mental health.

As a psychologist, father, and partner, I've witnessed both the joy of deep connection and the despair of disconnection. I've worked with countless individuals and couples who long for a loving connection but who feel isolated and defeated. Many are uncertain as to how to bridge the gap between wanting a better relationship and knowing how to create one. These personal and professional experiences led me to a pivotal question:

Why do some couples thrive while others struggle, even when both deeply want their relationship to succeed?

As I thought about this question, I wondered why some individuals are able to maintain a successful relationship throughout their lives, while others are unable to do so? What factors separate successful long-term relationships from those that fail? These questions led me to search for the factors behind those differences.

I soon discovered that many people assume that successful couples simply have a deeper love, are luckier, smarter, or have some special ability. As it turns out, these common assumptions are grossly inaccurate. As we shall see, successful relationships are not based on chance, but on more basic factors that underlie all relationships.

While numerous studies have explored the causes for relationship failure, their findings often provide only limited insights because of their focus on why relationships fail rather than what makes them succeed. There are very few studies focusing on couples in thriving long-term relationships to determine which qualities most contribute to relationship success.

To explore this issue more deeply, I conducted a comparative study of couples in long-term relationships—specifically those who had been together for over twenty years and described their relationships as strong, satisfying, or deeply fulfilling. These couples represented a wide range of ages, backgrounds, ethnicities, income levels, and lifestyles.

Surprisingly, thriving and distressed couples had much in common. Both groups fell in love, shared positive experiences, created memories together, and wanted their relationships to succeed. They both faced similar problems including issues involving money, children, extended family, work, health, and other common challenges and concerns.

The most significant finding of this study was that the success of a relationship rests upon specific "core" needs that are essential to all intimate relationships. A total of 16 core needs serve as the emotional and behavioral anchors that form the foundation of all relationships.

Each of these needs plays a pivotal role in the stability and health of a relationship. More importantly, these needs were found to be interconnected, forming a pattern that determined the overall strength of the relationship.

Couples in successful relationships understand these core needs and are much better at consistently meeting them, when compared to those in distressed relationships.

Thriving couples didn't possess better luck or some special gift— they simply met specific core needs more effectively and consistently. As a result, they are able to achieve a greater level of intimacy and satisfaction in their relationships.

Couples in distressed relationships, however, often struggle and experience much more conflict, not because they lack love or commitment, but because they do not recognize, express, or fulfill these needs effectively. Many relationship problems stem not from incompatibility, but from these unmet core needs.

When these essential needs go unrecognized or unfulfilled, disconnection and conflict follow, leading to the erosion of the relationship. On the other hand, when these needs are consistently met, relationships heal, grow, and intimacy deepens.

Another finding was how couples responded to challenges. Successful couples worked as a team, not as opponents or adversaries. Their approach was collaborative rather than hostile or confrontational. This pattern resulted in much less stress on the relationship.

Another key finding was that there is no "single" type of successful couple. They come from diverse backgrounds and often do not fit the stereotype of what many might think of as an ideal couple, based on their communication and behavior. Some communicate openly with warmth while others are much more reserved. Some can be emotionally intense while others are more laid-back.

What they share, however, is a unified commitment to protecting their relationship, along with consistent patterns of communication and behavior that meet core needs and reinforce emotional security and connection.

Many people in successful relationships had the advantage of parents who modeled effective relationship skills. Even when only one partner had this advantage it still had positive benefits to the relationship.

Unfortunately, many individuals do not have this advantage. Instead, others may have experienced family environments marked by conflict, neglect, and poor communication. As a result, they often had limited experience in managing conflict, meeting emotional needs, or effectively talking out problems.

Although these negative patterns can be a challenge to overcome, they are not permanent and can be replaced with more positive, healthy behavior that will significantly improve a relationship. Anyone with a desire to understand and practice the principles suggested in this book can create and maintain healthy, loving, long-term relationships.

Based on my research, I developed the *Relationship Wealth Model* —a framework that defines *Relationship Wealth* as the shared belief that one's relationship has meaningful emotional value, grounded in personal experiences and the consistent satisfaction of core relationship needs.

When these relationship needs are consistently met, they directly strengthen the emotional connection between partners. The model is grounded in the idea that lasting, successful relationships are not built by chance, but through the ongoing investment of intentional communication, meaningful behavior, and consistent care.

This book offers a practical, research-based blueprint for creating stronger, more fulfilling relationships. When couples learn to recognize and consistently meet their core relationship needs, they build a foundation for a strong, lasting, and more fulfilling relationship.

Inside this book, you'll find:

- A clear explanation of the 16 Core Needs that determine relationship wealth and satisfaction.
- Practical tools to help you recognize and meet those needs in yourself and your partner.
- The Relationship Wealth Scale, a self-assessment to help you identify your relationship's strengths and areas for growth.
- Real-life insights derived from couples who have overcome common challenges and built successful long-term partnerships.

The mission of this book is to provide more than just information— it's to provide a blueprint for building and sustaining successful long-term relationships. Drawing on the proven strategies of successful couples, this book will show you how to cultivate the deep intimacy and lasting satisfaction that you've been searching for.

With consistent and intentional effort, you can strengthen your bond and experience the many benefits of a healthy, rewarding partnership. In the chapters ahead, we'll explore the core needs that form the foundation of every successful relationship and provide practical tools for meeting them.

Whether you're in a committed relationship, just starting to date, recovering from loss, or beginning again, this book is for you. It's also for couples who are doing well overall but want to grow in specific areas—or who simply desire a deeper, more fulfilling connection.

You have the power to create a relationship that is strong, meaningful, and lasting. By learning the proven strategies of successful couples—and consistently putting them into practice—you can experience the deep and lasting rewards of what I call *Relationship Wealth*.

THE RELATIONSHIP
WEALTH MODEL

1

WHAT IS RELATIONSHIP WEALTH?

The relationships that we have with others are important because they add significant value to our overall quality of life. In a sense, our relationships can be viewed as a form of personal wealth, with each one enriching our lives in a unique way.

In today's world, many people focus on acquiring financial wealth and material possessions. Wealth is often measured by the amount of money a person has, the value of their investments, the size of their home, or their material assets. Those with this perspective tend to focus their time and energy on increasing material wealth, often overlooking other dimensions of wealth. However, in a broader sense, wealth includes much more than just financial and material assets.

Others believe that wealth is related to power, status, recognition, or fame. These individuals invest significant time and effort in advancing their careers or increasing their social standing.

Wealth can be defined in many ways, depending on an individual's perspective. It may include good health, happiness, security, meaningful work, spiritual fulfillment, and, of course, quality relationships. Each of these can serve as a primary source of wealth in life.

Wealth, like a tree with many branches, has many important dimensions. The trunk of the tree can be seen as the core of wealth – life itself. Without life, all other forms of wealth become meaningless. The main branches of wealth might include health, relationships, finances, career, and any activity seen as meaningful or valuable. Each branch holds unique significance and contributes to the overall quality of life.

Many people achieve great success in their careers or accumulate significant financial assets, yet still find themselves unhappy. Others may possess fame or physical beauty but remain chronically dissatisfied. History is full of examples of individuals who excelled in one area of life yet still experienced deep unhappiness. For many, this discontent leads to emotional despair rather than fulfillment, and can result in poor mental and physical health, substance abuse, and troubled relationships.

In contrast, there are those who may be financially poor but still feel deeply satisfied with the quality of their lives. Despite lacking financial wealth or material possessions, they find contentment through meaningful connections with others. One key reason for their happiness is that they have strong, fulfilling relationships that meet their emotional needs. In essence, they possess "relationship wealth."

Most people believe that each component of wealth is important and that, together, they create a more complete definition of true wealth. Many would likely agree that achieving the highest quality of life requires a balanced view of wealth rather than focusing too much on any one aspect of it.

This book focuses on the dimension of wealth found in relationships and its contribution to overall quality of life. This perspective is significant because it places considerable value on personal relationships. While relationships offer many benefits, their greatest advantage is the deep meaning, emotional security, and happiness they bring.

Relationships form a major part of personal wealth, serving as a primary source of meaning and satisfaction that enhances overall quality of life. Regardless of how much material wealth one accumulates, relationships make up a substantial share of the emotional meaning and satisfaction of a rich and meaningful life.

Relationship wealth extends beyond one's partner and includes all of one's social connections. An individual's network of relationships may include a spouse or partner, parents, children, siblings, friends, co-workers, and others. Much of a person's happiness in life comes from the satisfaction these relationships provide. Each connection contributes to one's overall sense of relationship wealth.

Although relationship wealth applies to all social relationships, the focus of this book will be on intimate partnerships. In this regard, the concept of "relationship wealth" can be defined as a couple's shared belief that their relationship holds significant positive value, based on their feelings, thoughts, and experiences. While each partner's perception is unique and shaped by personal experience, true relationship wealth requires mutual agreement that the relationship is of great value to both partners.

Relationships are continuously growing and evolving. While many may develop into lifelong relationships, many others will come and go, lasting only briefly. Unlike material possessions, relationships cannot be saved or stored away. Instead, they must be experienced through moments of shared connection. The quality of this connection can vary significantly but ultimately will affect the level of relationship wealth.

The perceived value of a relationship is an essential part of intimate relationships. This value is determined by the perception of each partner. When couples recognize and appreciate the value of their relationship, and feel that they truly matter to each other, the relationship is viewed as having significant value. This shared perception of value is the essence of relationship wealth.

Relationship wealth is built through emotional experiences that accumulate over time. Each emotional experience carries a specific value that contributes to the overall quality of the relationship. While a single experience may have an impact, the cumulative effect of many experiences significantly influences the depth and quality of a relationship. Shared experiences shape how each partner thinks, speaks, and behaves within the relationship.

Relationship wealth consists of a reservoir of shared experiences, feelings, thoughts, and memories. Each experience contributes to this reservoir and adds emotional depth and meaning to the relationship. Although relationship wealth is dynamic and evolves, it remains relatively stable overall because it is rooted more in past experiences than in the present state of the relationship. However, the quality of those past experiences plays a critical role in maintaining this stability.

Relationship wealth fluctuates primarily on how well core relationship needs are met. The consistent satisfaction of these essential needs fuel positive emotions and thoughts that contribute to building relationship wealth. In essence, a couple's ability to meet these core relationship needs directly impacts the level and quality of relationship wealth. Relationship wealth is continuously shaped by the satisfaction of needs. When relationship needs are met, relationship wealth grows. When the level of satisfaction decreases, relationship wealth declines.

Most people can generally estimate their level of relationship wealth. When asked whether their relationship is strong, they can typically answer right away. This is because they maintain an ongoing awareness of their satisfaction with their relationship. This awareness draws from a reservoir of current and past experiences, emotions, and thoughts that together capture the overall value of the relationship.

Accurately measuring relationship wealth is challenging because perceptions of its value are subjective. However, one way to assess it is with a scale that measures satisfaction with regard to core relationship needs. The Relationship Wealth Scale serves as a valuable tool for evaluating overall relationship quality. However, it is best to view the results as insights into where the relationship can grow and improve, rather than as judgments about what is wrong with the relationship. Details of this scale can be found in Appendix B.

Past emotional and relationship experiences are significant

because they often have a lasting effect, whether positive or negative. Even if these experiences happened long ago, the emotions associated with them can still influence the present and future. This phenomenon, in which past feelings and emotions continue to shape a relationship over time, can be described as 'emotional radiation.' These experiences, positive or negative, can resonate long after they occur, and shape the quality of the relationship. This typically occurs when a significant event is tied to strong emotions. For example, a marriage proposal usually creates positive feelings. When recalled from memory later, those positive emotions can resurface because the event and its emotions are stored together in memory.

In general, the more intense an emotional experience, the longer its impact lasts. An important benefit of this process is that positive feelings can continue to radiate and help to sustain the relationship's quality and stability. These accumulated positive emotions provide a supportive foundation for the relationship. For example, couples often reminisce about shared pleasurable experiences, which reactivates those positive feelings and reinforces the relationship's value.

The cumulative effect of past positive emotions is essential to relationship wealth. Without this cumulative effect, sustaining a relationship would be extremely difficult because intimate relationships are built upon layers of experiences. In essence, these past positive experiences are critical for establishing a strong foundation and maintaining the relationship's health and stability.

Just as positive emotional experiences build and sustain relationship wealth, negative emotional experiences can diminish it. The more significant the negative event, the greater its impact. Past negative events can radiate strong emotions long after they occur. For example, pain from a failed relationship can linger and can radiate negativity that affects future relationships.

Negative emotions often have a stronger, more lasting impact on a relationship than positive ones. Because negative emotions tend to be more enduring, they can have a stronger negative effect on a relationship. Their enduring nature can also diminish the enjoyment of positive emotional experiences. Although quality relationships thrive on positive emotional experiences, they must also be able to withstand the stresses of daily life.

A single negative emotional experience can outweigh multiple positive ones. For example, a couple might spend an enjoyable day together sharing many positive moments but later have an argument in which one partner says something hurtful to the other. In this situation, negative emotions are likely to linger and overshadow earlier positive feelings.

A single argument, disagreement, or event can cause significant harm to a relationship. However, most conflicts do not necessarily result in lasting damage. More often, the accumulation of negative experiences causes the most harm, especially when they outweigh the positive experiences.

Since negative emotions last longer and have a greater impact, it is essential to prevent or resolve issues quickly to avoid long-term damage. When strong negative emotions persist, relationship quality and stability decline. This strain is cumulative and can erode the relationship, and lead to "relationship poverty."

Relationship poverty, unlike relationship wealth, is the accumulation of negative emotions, thoughts, and memories that creates a negative perception of the relationship's value. These negative experiences not only harm the relationship but also disrupt the positive emotions needed to sustain it. When negative emotions persist, maintaining a positive perception of the relationship becomes increasingly difficult. As relationship poverty deepens, the desire to resolve issues decreases. At this stage, the relationship deteriorates further, which makes it even harder to sustain.

Couples in successful relationships highly value their relationships and consistently strive to maintain a quality connection. Like financial wealth, relationship wealth grows through investments of time, attention, security, and communication. In essence, everything partners say and do is a potential investment in building relationship wealth.

Great relationships take time and effort to develop. However, building a quality relationship requires the right tools and strategies to effectively meet its core relationship needs. Meeting these core relationship needs increases relationship wealth and provides the many benefits of an emotionally satisfying long-term relationship. In the next chapter, the core relationship needs that serve as the foundation of all intimate relationships will be explored.

2

THE CORE RELATIONSHIP NEEDS

Relationship wealth is built on the accumulation of positive feelings, thoughts, and shared experiences over time. The primary source of relationship wealth stems from the successful fulfillment of each partner's needs. The degree to which these needs are met directly affects the value that each partner attributes to the relationship.

Relationship science has shown that when individuals feel closely connected, understood, and cared for by their partners, their need for relatedness is fulfilled (Ryan and Deci, 2018). The role of need satisfaction in intimate relationships has been extensively studied. Research shows that individuals have basic relationship needs that, when satisfied, motivate them to stay together as a couple. The fulfillment of these needs is directly associated with greater relationship quality, commitment, and shared intimacy. The need for connection, love, and belonging is deeply intertwined with intimacy in intimate relationships. This basic human need for connection significantly affects the depth, quality, and longevity of relationships.

The concept of building and sustaining relationship wealth is founded on the principle of need satisfaction. When the core needs of a relationship are met, its quality and stability improve. Building and maintaining a successful long-term relationship requires understanding the core needs that form its foundation. Meeting these needs ensures its stability, quality, and longevity.

Studies have identified a variety of needs that must be satisfied to achieve a successful relationship. For example, the need for love, trust, and effective communication are often cited as essential to a quality relationship. A limitation of many studies, however, is that they focus on only a select number of needs rather than on the full spectrum of needs essential to building and maintaining a successful relationship.

When specifically examining successful relationships, it becomes clear that they are based on a broader and more extensive set of needs, each of which contributes to the overall stability and quality of the relationship. This more comprehensive perspective on relationship needs provides a deeper understanding of the core factors necessary for maintaining a long-term, successful relationship.

Relationship Wealth is based on 16 core relationship needs that form the foundation of a successful intimate relationship. These core needs form the backbone of a healthy relationship and are crucial to its functioning. Each core need plays an indispensable role in determining the overall quality of the relationship.

Core Relationship Needs

Emotional Needs

Love
Nurturance
Pleasure
Security

Foundation Needs

Communication
Trust

Respect
Honesty
Loyalty
Leadership
Teamwork
Commitment
Fairness
Friendship

Problem Solving Needs

Analysis
Solutions

Stress Management Needs

Core relationship needs are fundamental to all intimate relationships, and they form the foundation for their growth and longevity. The health and stability of a relationship are directly related to how effectively each partner meets these essential needs. The extent to which these needs are met will have a direct impact on the overall quality of the relationship.

For an intimate relationship to thrive, each partner must consistently meet the other's core needs. It would be difficult to imagine a healthy relationship where love, trust, communication, or security are lacking.

Couples in successful relationships not only recognize the significance of these core needs but also make a consistent effort to meet them in satisfying ways. In contrast, couples in distressed relationships often fail to meet one or more of these needs, either due to a lack of understanding of their significance or insufficient knowledge of how to meet them effectively.

Defining what constitutes a "successful" relationship can be challenging. One perspective is that success is determined by the level of contentment or satisfaction that a couple experiences that leads them to want to stay together. According to this view, the relationship may be satisfying in some areas while merely functional in others. Despite its limitations and occasional dissatisfaction, there is an overall acceptance of the relationship by the partners. The key idea here is that, for the relationship to be considered successful, the level of satisfaction derived from certain needs must outweigh any dissatisfaction caused by unmet needs.

Another perspective is that a successful relationship is one in which both partners feel that their needs are met at a satisfying level. While unmet needs may be tolerable for a time, there must be mutual agreement on how these needs will be addressed for the relationship to be considered truly successful. Couples in long-term, high-quality relationships often believe that, generally, meeting all of the core relationship needs is essential for a successful relationship.

For many couples, relationship satisfaction falls on a spectrum which ranges from a minimal level of contentment to complete fulfillment. In essence, relationship satisfaction exists on a continuum, with the level of contentment determined by how well each partner meets the other's needs.

Although couples can often function for a time without every need being met, prolonged neglect of any core need can erode the quality and stability of the relationship. For example, if one partner is overwhelmed with multiple responsibilities, they may be less available to meet their partner's needs. This situation is usually understood by most couples and is generally tolerated, especially when these needs have been consistently satisfied in the past.

When relationship needs go unmet for extended periods, they can become a significant source of stress and gradually weaken the foundation of the relationship. This pattern often leads to increased negative emotions, which results in decreased relationship stability and quality. If left unaddressed the relationship may become strained, and the likelihood of failure increases.

Relationship needs are not rigid but are dynamic and adapt to changing circumstances over time. For instance, the need for affection, love, and security may shift depending on life events and other needs. Similarly, physical intimacy often evolves over the course of a relationship. In the early stages, sexual intimacy may be frequent, but over time, factors such as health, energy level, and life responsibilities can influence its frequency. Understanding and adapting to these changes is a necessary part of maintaining a healthy long-term relationship.

As indicated, the underlying structure of an intimate relationship is built on a foundation of core relationship needs. Each of these needs serves as a pillar supporting the relationship. However, successful relationships are based not just on the satisfaction of individual needs, but on their interconnection. In essence, the real strength lies in the connections between these core needs and how they interact to reinforce the relationship.

The interconnection of relationship needs is essential to the structure of the relationship but, more importantly, this interconnection creates a dynamic process that further strengthens the relationship. This interactive effect is based on the idea that the satisfaction or dissatisfaction of any one need impacts other needs. For example, an increase in affection may increase a partner's sense of security, trust, or pleasure. Conversely, a lack of honesty can diminish that partner's sense of trust and security in the relationship. This dynamic interplay of needs plays a critical role in the health and stability of intimate relationships.

This dynamic interaction between needs creates a synergy that provides strength and stability to the relationship. When one core relationship need is unsatisfied, it creates a ripple effect that can influence other needs in a negative way. In essence, any significant change in the satisfaction level of one need has the potential to impact others. This effect is cumulative and contributes significantly to the overall level of relationship wealth.

Another major benefit of this interactive process is its protective effect on the relationship. When the satisfaction level of one or more needs is insufficient, other satisfied needs may help compensate for the deficiency. In essence, the cumulative effect of satisfied needs serves as a buffer against the negative impact of less satisfied needs.

For example, one partner may not express as much affection as the other would like, yet that partner may satisfy every other need. In this case, the overall level of satisfaction of other needs helps to compensate for the unsatisfied need. And just as there is an interactive effect within the relationship, there is also an interactive effect between partners. As one partner meets the other's needs, there will often be a reciprocal response, which prompts the other partner to meet their needs in return. In essence, one partner's efforts to meet core relationship needs may influence the other partner's willingness to do the same.

It is important for relationship needs to be satisfied in a predictable and consistent manner. Achieving this requires each partner to learn what the other partner needs in order to feel satisfied within the relationship. Understanding each other's needs and desires is essential for maintaining a fulfilling long-term relationship. However, it is important to remember that what satisfies one partner may not be as satisfying for the other. For example, one partner may desire more affection than the other, which can lead to frustration or conflict. Establishing clear expectations regarding each other's needs helps prevent potential conflicts and problems in the relationship.

Each core relationship need will be more fully described in later chapters, as well as effective strategies for meeting these needs. The goal is first to gain a better understanding of each need and then to learn effective strategies to satisfy them. By developing a successful approach to meeting relationship needs, couples can build relationship wealth and enjoy the many benefits of a fulfilling, long-lasting relationship.

3

RELATIONSHIP ZONES

As previously indicated, the basic structure of all intimate relationships is built on a foundation of sixteen core needs. Each need contributes to the overall health and stability of a relationship. Relationship needs can be grouped together based on similar purpose or function. In this context, each need falls into one of four distinct groups or "zones." Each zone represents a specific phase of interaction, depending on the specific needs that are being addressed. These phases of interaction serve to create, build, and preserve relationship wealth.

Organizing relationship needs into distinct zones helps illustrate the structure of intimate relationships and highlights their strengths and weaknesses. This approach serves as a guide for couples to understand their needs and can enable them to focus on improving their relationship. In essence, relationship zones provide a practical framework for more effectively meeting relationship needs.

In order to achieve greater clarity in distinguishing one zone from another, a different color is used for each of the four zones. For this purpose, the colors blue, green, yellow, and red will be used. In this system, each colored zone represents a combination of needs serving a similar purpose.

The relationship needs in the Blue Zone include love, nurturance, pleasure, and security. These emotional needs are the primary reason couples seek intimate relationships. Each of these needs contributes to positive emotions, which serve as the primary source of energy that sustains relationships. In essence, the Blue Zone is the heart of the relationship and is where the largest part of relationship wealth is derived.

The Green Zone consists of structural needs that form the foundation and backbone of a relationship. These needs include communication, trust, respect, honesty, loyalty, teamwork, leadership, commitment, fairness, and friendship. The Green Zone is where couples spend most of their time. Activities such as eating meals, watching television, doing chores, and most conversations take place in this zone.

The Yellow Zone is the phase in which problems and conflicts are addressed. This is where issues are defined, solutions are suggested, and agreements are made. It is where the more serious challenges affecting the relationship are addressed. These may include issues related to the personal distress of either partner, relationship conflicts, or external stress-related issues. Problems, by their nature, are often associated with increased emotion. As a result, this zone is often where some degree of emotional stress is experienced.

The Red Zone is the phase in which the relationship is in serious distress. In this zone, one or both partners may become emotionally overwhelmed. During this phase, emotions can overtake reason, which can lead to communication or behavior that damages the relationship. Although stress is a common reaction to problems, in this case emotional reactions become uncontrolled, and can lead to destructive arguments and behavior that can critically harm the relationship.

The Red Zone is often where the most harm occurs in relationships. When emotional reactions escalate into toxic communication and behavior, the health and stability of the relationship are at risk. Effectively managing these harmful patterns is essential for protecting the health and stability of the relationship. Strategies for achieving this will be addressed in a following chapter.

Relationship zones, and their core needs, provide a framework for understanding the essential elements of an intimate relationship. This framework serves as a blueprint that illustrates how each need, and the interactions between them, contribute to the long-term health and stability of a relationship. This "relationship blueprint" provides a picture of both the structure and dynamic nature of an intimate relationship. This is essential for building and maintaining a strong relationship. The following graphic illustrates the relationship zones and the needs within them.

THE RELATIONSHIP ZONES

BLUE ZONE

Love
Nurturance
Pleasure
Security

GREEN ZONE

Communication
Trust
Respect
Honesty
Loyalty
Teamwork
Leadership
Commitment
Fairness
Friendship

YELLOW ZONE

Problem Solving Skills

RED ZONE

Relationship Stress Management

Each need can influence and have an impact on other needs. Just as a change in one need can affect others, a shift in one relationship zone can influence changes in other zones. Negative emotions originating in the Red Zone can significantly affect emotional needs within the Blue Zone. For example, if a couple has a painful argument that leaves one partner feeling emotionally hurt, it may lead to a decrease in security and physical intimacy.

Prolonged periods of time struggling in the Red Zone can decrease a couple's desire to meet each other's needs for love, nurturance, pleasure, or security within the Blue Zone. This decreased level of affection and positive support within the Blue Zone may lead to a decrease in the desire or motivation to work together to solve problems. As a result, problems remain unresolved, emotional stress accumulates, and an unhealthy pattern of interaction causes further deterioration in the relationship.

Through an understanding of relationship zones and the needs within them, couples can focus more directly on their specific areas of need. This refined approach can help couples meet needs more efficiently and strategically while avoiding unnecessary roadblocks or distractions.

Although each need within a zone plays a significant role in an intimate relationship, certain needs are universal and span all relationship zones. Communication is a primary example of a universal need because it plays an active role in all the needs within each zone. It is essential for expressing love, resolving problems, reaching agreements, and addressing everyday issues. In essence, communication is intricately linked to all relationship needs across every relationship zone.

The time spent in each relationship zone varies for every couple and largely depends on their needs. Each couple has a unique pattern of interaction based on the time spent in each zone. There are, of course, many variations in these patterns of interaction. The quality of a relationship is often reflected in the time spent in each zone. The pattern or distribution of time across zones is often significantly different between successful and distressed couples.

Successful Versus Distressed Relationships

Successful couples generally spend more time in the Blue Zone than distressed couples. They express love and affection more frequently and are better able to meet their needs for love, intimacy, nurturance, pleasure, and security. Additionally, they are generally more receptive to their partner's desire for intimacy.

Couples in distressed relationships, as one might expect, often spend less time interacting within the Blue Zone. As a result, they frequently feel unloved, dissatisfied, and more insecure in the relationship. Ongoing negative emotions and tension often interfere with or limit the expression of love, intimacy, pleasure, security, and other positive emotions. This diminished desire to express love, affection, or nurturance frequently leads to further emotional distress and dissatisfaction in the relationship.

Most of the time that couples spend together is in the Green Zone, where they meet the everyday needs and responsibilities of life. For successful couples, the Green Zone is typically a stable and positive phase of interactions marked by stability and cooperation. For distressed couples, the Green Zone reflects varying degrees of stability and peace. Although there may be some periods of satisfaction and lower stress in this zone, underlying tension, uncertainty, and general dissatisfaction often exist in the background.

When addressing problems in the Yellow Zone, successful couples devote adequate time to address their conflicts and issues. They emphasize focused listening and utilize effective problem-solving skills. They are also more aware of their emotions, particularly anger, which they understand can cause harm to their relationship. On the other hand, distressed couples generally spend more time in the Yellow Zone due to a lack of effective problem-solving skills or an inability to tolerate stress. Discussing emotionally stressful issues is often challenging for distressed couples. Difficulty controlling emotions frequently escalates frustration, which can lead to further conflict and stress.

Couples in successful relationships rarely enter the Red Zone, as they understand the importance of protecting their relationship. When one partner becomes overwhelmed with emotion or begins to drift into the Red Zone, the other partner often takes the initiative to disengage to allow for a cooling off period. Couples in distressed relationships, however, often do not have adequate safeguards to prevent their emotions from escalating. Consequently, they more often enter the Red Zone where they engage in harmful communication or behavior.

When this happens, significant damage to the relationship can occur. It is important to note that once emotional injury or harm occurs, these negative thoughts and emotions can linger long after the conflict has ended. In essence, harm to the relationship not only occurs during the conflict but can also continue long afterward.

The Interaction of Zones

Problems in one relationship zone often have an impact on other zones. For example, time spent in the Red Zone directly affects the amount of time likely to be spent in the Blue Zone. Once anger or hurt occurs in the Red Zone, sharing feelings of love, nurturance, or pleasure in the Blue Zone becomes extremely difficult. Instead, feelings of insecurity, anxiety, and resentment may persist.

Couples in successful relationships generally maintain a consistent and predictable pattern of interaction within each relationship zone, moving smoothly from one zone to another. In contrast, couples in distressed relationships tend to be more unpredictable and inconsistent in their interactions, frequently fluctuating between periods of conflict and stability. This instability contributes to greater insecurity in the relationship.

Effectively meeting the needs within each relationship zone helps build and maintain relationship wealth. Understanding the relationship zones and the needs within them provides a valuable framework for creating and enhancing intimate relationships. In essence, this understanding enables couples to create a practical blueprint to guide their relationship toward health, stability, greater satisfaction, and relationship wealth.

All relationships have the potential to change and grow. By applying the strategies outlined in the following chapters, any couple can learn to effectively meet their relationship's needs and make the relationship stronger and more satisfying over time. This strategic approach builds relationship wealth and leads to a more successful and fulfilling long-term relationship.

THE BLUE ZONE

4

LOVE
MORE THAN A FEELING!

Of all the core relationship needs in the Blue Zone, love is the most essential. The foundation of every successful intimate relationship is the ability to express and receive love. This need is the primary reason that couples commit to long term relationships, yet many struggle to clearly define what love truly is.

"Love' is a broad term that applies to various types of relationships. There is love for a partner, which is the focus here, as well as love for parents, children, siblings, and friends. The term is also used loosely to refer to love for objects, interests, or causes. However, the love shared with an intimate partner is unique and distinctly different from all other forms of love.

Defining the precise meaning of love is challenging. Many writers, poets, and others have attempted to describe its nature, but there is no single definition that encompasses everyone's understanding, expectations, or experiences. Love is expressed and felt in countless ways, and each person holds their own unique view on what love is. Each of us has our own individual understanding and experience of what love is and what it means to us.

One definition of love may describe it love as a deep affection, attraction, or devotion toward another person. It involves the positive feelings and thoughts that draw people to each other and help sustain a bond over time. In essence, love consists of emotions and beliefs that together create the experience known as love.

Several theories have attempted to describe romantic love, one of which is the Triangular Theory of Love (Steinberg, 1988). This theory proposes that love comprises three components: intimacy, passion, and commitment. Intimacy refers to emotional closeness and connection within a loving relationship. Passion involves the motivation and arousal associated with sexual attraction and the desire to satisfy sexual needs. Commitment represents the decision to remain with a partner in a long-term relationship.

Sue Johnson (2008) describes love and emotional engagement as fundamental human needs, essential for well-being and trust. It is a basic survival code in which the bonds of love form a secure emotional attachment that serves as the foundation of a lasting, fulfilling relationship. This view is rooted in attachment theory where love and emotional closeness is dependent upon a secure engagement with one's partner.

Most descriptions of love encompass four interrelated levels: emotional, physical, sensory, and cognitive. On an emotional level, love is marked by feelings of warmth and contentment. Physically, it includes the pleasure from touch and intimacy. At the sensory level, there is the pleasure of seeing a partner or hearing their voice. And on a cognitive level, love involves positive thoughts and beliefs about one's partner, enriching the experience of love.

The foundation of an intimate relationship is built on the shared experience of physical attraction, mutual positive feelings, and a mutual desire to be together. When these elements align, they foster genuine connection, laying the groundwork for deeper intimacy to develop.

Love is neither static nor stagnant. Instead, it is a dynamic emotional experience that evolves over time. Typically, love is flexible and adapts to changing needs and circumstances. While intimacy and passion may ebb and flow, love can remain strong and stable over time.

Love often begins with an attraction between two people based on a combination of physical appearance, shared interests, similar values, or the mysterious factor referred to as "chemistry." Over time, these positive feelings deepen and grow, which are recognized as love by each partner. Positive and satisfying emotional experiences reinforce this bond and sustain the desire for long-term commitment.

Attraction can be immediate or develop gradually. Initially, attraction factors dominant the emotional experience of love. Over time, as partners' needs are consistently met, a deeper love grows, grounded in shared experiences and a unified commitment to the relationship.

Love can be understood as consisting of two main components: feeling loved and expressing love. The development, growth, and long-term stability of an intimate relationship rely on the interplay of these two aspects. While they interact closely, each has its own distinct qualities. The way in which love is expressed and experienced can vary greatly. Although these two components of love function interactively, each one has its own unique characteristics. The expression of love will be explored more extensively in the next chapter.

The experience of feeling loved has been deeply desired throughout history. People have sought love for companionship, emotional intimacy, passion, sexual desire, pleasure, and feelings of attachment and belonging. Many also long for a partner with whom they can share feelings, thoughts, and experiences and who unconditionally accepts them, or who can empathize with their experiences of joy and suffering. Each person's experience of love is unique, and is influenced by individual desires, expectations, and life experiences.

While most people can recognize when they feel loved, they are often less aware of whether their partner feels the same. Each person brings their own expectations, desires, and perceptions to the relationship. A lack of understanding about what a partner needs to feel loved is a primary factor in relationship dissatisfaction.

A common misconception is that a partner should "automatically" know how to meet the other partner's emotional needs for feeling loved. Many people assume that their partner shares all of their beliefs about love, which often leads to misunderstandings and conflict. When expectations go unmet, frustration and discontent are likely to occur. To avoid this, it is essential for partners to openly discuss their individual needs and preferences for feeling loved.

Beyond knowing what makes one feel loved, it is also important to understand how much love is needed to feel satisfied. Each person has unique expectations for how they would like to receive love from their partner. For example, one partner might want to hear "I love you" several times a day, while the other may be content hearing it less frequently. One might prefer a lot of affection, while the other may be indifferent to it. These differences can be a significant source of stress in a relationship. For love to be satisfying to both partners, there must be a clear understanding of each other's needs, which can only be achieved through open and honest communication.

A key difference between couples in successful relationships and those in distressed ones is the ability to openly communicate their needs for feeling loved. Although this requires emotional vulnerability, it fosters a deeper level of intimacy between partners. Couples who can share their needs in this way often experience a stronger sense of security and higher relationship quality.

In conclusion, the intimate experience of love is one of life's universally desired and greatest pleasures. While love is often described in similar terms by many couples, each relationship's unique needs and expectations create a distinct experience of love. At its core, love is the most important element of a quality and fulfilling long-term relationship. But for love to be enduring, it must be replenished and nurtured. The time and effort invested in building a loving relationship is small compared to the profound benefits of sharing a meaningful and fulfilling relationship. In the next chapter our focus will be on nurturance and the expression of love.

5

INTIMACY AND NURTURANCE
THE NOURISHING POWER OF LOVE

A mong all of the needs in a relationship, love is the most essential need for building a successful long-term relationship. However, for love to be sustained over time, it must be expressed and shared through nurturance. Nurturance is deeply intertwined with love and serves as the lifeblood of a successful relationship. While love consists of the feelings and beliefs that bond two people, nurturance is the life-support system that nourishes and enriches that bond. Love and nurturance are interdependent. Without one, the other cannot thrive.

Successful relationships require ongoing nurturance to be durable and healthy. The mutual exchange of love is the foundation of intimate relationships among successful couples. Like other relationship needs, nurturance is essential for maintaining a healthy bond. It provides a consistent flow of care and support that sustains and strengthens love, over time. These acts of care and love are the essence of a relationship in the Blue Zone.

Nurturance refers to the affection, attention, and actions that reinforce a positive connection between partners. It includes all the words and behavior that intimate partners express to each other that nourish and maintain a healthy relationship. Every relationship needs a minimum level of nurturance to remain strong and healthy. Nurturance typically involves what one partner says or does to express love and care for the other. When nurturance is shared and expressed by both partners it results in a deeper level of intimacy. The distinction between the two is that nurturance is what one partner gives to the other, while intimacy involves a reciprocal and shared exchange of nurturance between partners.

Points of Connection

On any given day, there are periods when partners communicate and interact with each other to express their thoughts, feelings, and needs. These moments of interaction form the basic unit of every relationship. Relationships cannot function or exist without them. The quality of these interactions or points of connection directly impacts the overall quality of a relationship. Each point of interaction requires active engagement between partners. Merely being present in the same space is not sufficient. For instance, a couple silently watching television together are not necessarily interacting with each other.

Whenever one partner engages with the other and receives a response, a connection is established. Each of these connection points serves a purpose, whether to express a need, make a request, share information, or simply connect. The primary function of these connection points is to address the basic needs of one or both partners. Each interaction helps partners to support one another and meet each other's needs.

Most couples connect in one or more interactions each day, with the frequency often influenced by individual needs. The greater the need, the more likely that an interaction will occur. These connections can range in duration from just a few seconds to several minutes or even longer. On average, the amount of time that couples spend actively interacting with each other daily has been estimated to be between thirty and sixty minutes (Sloan, 2001). Again, this can vary significantly depending on the needs of each couple.

The length and quality of time spent during each interaction plays a significant role in a couple's ability to meet their needs. In fact, the quality of each connection, rather than the quantity, is the strongest predictor of relationship satisfaction. It is important for each partner to recognize the value of these points of connection because the life of the relationship flows through this connection. Unfortunately, many couples take these connection points for granted and do not give them the attention needed. Maintaining this awareness is essential for improving the quality of the connection and building relationship wealth.

As previously noted, all communication flows through these connection points for the purpose of meeting each partner's needs in the relationship. The flow of nurturance and shared intimacy within these interactions is vital to the emotional enrichment, durability, and health of a relationship. Ultimately, the quality of nurturance that flows through these points determines the overall health, quality, and wealth of the relationship.

If a couple spends relatively little time each day interacting each day, the amount of time they dedicate to expressing nurturance is often even less. While many interactions can be measured in minutes, the expression of nurturance often is measured in seconds. Simple gestures, such as saying "I love you," or sharing a warm embrace, require minimal time and effort, yet are essential for a quality relationship. These brief but meaningful moments of nurturance and intimacy play an essential role in developing and sustaining a high-quality emotional connection. Over time, these acts of nurturance accumulate, and significantly influence the relationship's growth, stability, and quality.

Although expressing nurturance in a relationship requires very little time, many relationships are significantly "under-nurtured." In distressed relationships, a lack of nurturance often underlies many other relationship problems. The frustration caused by this lack of nurturance and intimacy places considerable stress on the relationship, making it difficult to maintain a healthy and stable connection. Several factors may contribute to why so many relationships are under-nurtured. For example, some individuals may not fully under-stand the importance of nurturance or have never learned how to express it effectively. Additionally, those who experienced a lacked nurturance during childhood often struggle to express it as adults.

Some people view nurturance as a sign of vulnerability, fearing it makes them appear overly dependent or weak. This perception often creates emotional barriers, leaving many unaware of the critical role nurturance plays in building healthy relationships. As a result, these relationships can suffer from a lack of emotional engagement and satisfaction.

Every relationship requires a minimum level of nurturance that meets each partner's needs. However, the amount of nurturance needed can vary significantly between partners, with one sometimes having a greater need than the other. Typically, individuals tend to provide nurturance in line with their own needs, mistakenly assuming their partner's desires reflect their own. This difference often leads to dissatisfaction, particularly for the partner who desires more nurturance than they receive.

Differences in the need for nurturance can be a significant source of conflict in relationships. The greater the difference between each partner's needs, the higher the likelihood of unhappiness and dissat-isfaction. Additionally, the need for nurturance is not static and can vary over time. For instance, a partner experiencing significant personal challenges or distress may need more nurturance and support than usual. In essence, the need for nurturance and intimacy is dynamic and can vary significantly depending on the needs of each partner.

Channels of Intimacy

The flow of nurturance between partners is the essence of an inti-mate, loving relationship. How couples express love and caring to each other has been described in a variety of ways. One model describes how couples express love through different languages, and that by understanding each partner's specific "love language" they can establish greater intimacy in their relationship (Chapman, 2015). This model helps couples align their expressions or languages of love to more effectively meet each other's needs.

The model presented in this chapter outlines three primary channels, or pathways, through which love is expressed between partners in an intimate relationship. These include the communication, physical, and behavioral channels. Each channel of intimacy can include a variety of expressions, each contributing to a healthy pattern of care in the relationship. These patterns can differ significantly between couples, shaped by their unique needs and desires. What matters most is that each expression of love is satisfying to both partners, and that the frequency and quality of nurturance meet each partner's need to feel loved.

Communication

The first and perhaps most important channel of intimacy is communication. This channel includes talking, listening, and nonverbal expressions of nurturance. Verbal expressions of love and nurturance are the most direct way to build relationship wealth and intimacy. There are countless ways that partners can express love through words, such as offering compliments, giving encouragement, providing praise, expressing appreciation, offering support, or by simply saying "I love you."

Listening is another essential aspect of communication that conveys love and nurturance. When one partner gives their full attention to the other without interruption or distraction, it is often viewed as a meaningful form of care and nurturance. An example of this is when a partner turns toward the other, focusing completely on what is being said. In essence, listening is a form of nurturance that is as essential to an intimate relationship as speaking, as it conveys value and respect for the speaking partner.

Intimacy and nurturance also can be communicated nonverbally through facial expressions, tone of voice, and gestures. A simple smile, nod, or maintaining eye contact while listening can be nurturing to one's partner. Nonverbal expressions of nurturance, particularly when combined with other forms of care, can significantly enhance the quality of love in an intimate relationship.

The following examples highlight the diverse ways in which love can be expressed in the communication channel.

- Expressing words of caring such as "I love you," or "I'm glad that you are in my life."
- Statements of appreciation
- Use of humor to express caring, hope, or for managing stress
- Listening with full attention
- Sharing ideas, hopes, and dreams
- Providing reassurance
- Supporting a partner who is feeling insecure
- Giving words of encouragement
- Providing emotional support
- Offering praise
- Giving compliments
- Expressing positive recognition in social situations

Physical Intimacy

The second channel of intimacy is expressed on a physical level. Physical intimacy consists of all forms of physical affection, including sexual intimacy, holding hands, hugging, or providing a back rub or a massage. Any physical behavior or gesture that conveys care and affection can be considered an expression of nurturance through the physical channel. The foundation of physical intimacy lies in expressions of affection and caring. This nurturance requires physical touch and conveys a powerful emotional connection that deepens the bond between partners.

The most significant form of physical nurturance is sexual intimacy. Expressions of sexual desire and intimacy play a major role in demonstrating love between partners and are essential for a healthy and satisfying relationship. Most successful couples derive significant pleasure from their sexual relationship and prioritize this aspect of their connection. Numerous resources are available to help couples build and enhance their sexual relationship (Joannides, 2021; Nagoski, 2015; Comfort, 2009).

Sexual intimacy holds profound meaning for most couples. The pleasure and emotional connection experienced in a satisfying sexual relationship are often a major source of relationship satisfaction. However, although sexuality is a natural and healthy part of an intimate relationship, it can also be a source of stress for many couples. Discussing sexual issues is challenging for many couples, making it one of the most common areas of conflict in relationships. A lack of communication about sexual needs, desires, and preferences frequently leads to partner dissatisfaction, which can set the stage for relationship problems. In fact, frustration and distress related to unmet sexual needs are among the primary reasons for relationship failure.

One of the most common sources of tension in relationships is a mismatch in sexual desire between partners. This difference can become a major issue, as it is often misinterpreted as a measure of attraction or love, even though this is frequently not the case. Addressing these sensitive subjects requires care, empathy, and mutual understanding.

The frequency and quality of sexual intimacy often vary significantly between partners, particularly over time. Because individual needs differ greatly, it is essential for both partners to communicate openly about their sexual needs and desires. When these needs are acknowledged and respected, intimacy becomes more fulfilling and gratifying. However, when sexual differences are not addressed, it can place significant stress on the relationship, resulting in feelings of anxiety, inadequacy, and self-doubt, which make discussion about these issues even more difficult.

Past negative sexual experiences can further complicate communication about sexual needs and concerns. Many individuals carry negative beliefs or emotions from prior relationships that strain their current sexual relationship, leading them to avoid discussing these critical issues. However, avoiding these conversations only deepens the conflict and dissatisfaction. Instead, it is essential that couples strive to define and express their individual needs in order to create a more satisfying and supportive sexual engagement between them.

In cases involving a history of sexual abuse or trauma, navigating these challenges requires an even greater level of support and understanding. Seeking the guidance of a qualified professional experienced in addressing sexual issues can be beneficial in helping couples resolve these complex issues.

The following examples highlight the diverse ways in which physical intimacy can be expressed:

- Physical affection
- Sexual intimacy
- Holding hands
- Kissing
- Touch
- Hugging
- Back rubs
- Massages

Behavioral Nurturance

The third channel of nurturance is expressed through behaviors or actions that convey care and affection. Behavioral nurturance includes any behavior or action that communicates love and caring. This can include a wide variety of acts that show care from one partner to another. Examples include helping with chores, preparing meals, giving flowers, performing acts of kindness, or planning a date night. The possibilities are limited only by the creativity of each couple.

Additionally, behavioral nurturance can involve any action that reduces a partner's stress. Examples include taking on extra responsibilities when a partner is overwhelmed, assisting with tasks, or exercising self-control in words and emotions during times of conflict. Any action that reduces a partner's stress serves as a meaningful expression of behavioral nurturance.

The following examples highlight the diverse ways in which intimacy can be expressed through behavior:

- Doing things for one's partner
- Helping with responsibilities and chores
- Sharing activities together
- Taking care of one's partner when ill
- Responding to requests in a positive way
- Being protective
- Creating playfulness / laughter
- Using nonverbal behavior – eye contact, a smile, paying full attention
- Giving gifts
- Sharing resources
- Performing actions that ensure safety and security
- Spending time together
- Performing acts of kindness
- Inhibiting negative emotions
- Controlling personal stress
- Reducing stress on one's partner

Nurturance in Successful Relationships

As the above examples illustrate, nurturance can be expressed in many ways. Each couple develops a unique pattern of intimacy and nurturance, which naturally evolves over the course of their relationship. These expressions of nurturance and love often form a predictable and recurring pattern. The quality of a couple's intimacy pattern directly influences each partner's satisfaction with the relationship. In essence, the level of fulfillment provided by their nurturance pattern is a critical factor in the long-term health, and wealth, of the relationship.

One key difference between couples in successful relationships and those in distressed relationships is the quality of their nurturance pattern. Couples in successful relationships tend to have a positive and satisfying pattern of nurturance. They consistently try to nurture each other daily, expressing love and care through multiple channels in meaningful and satisfying ways. More importantly, their nurturance pattern is tailored to their partner's specific needs, which generally leads to greater relationship satisfaction and stability.

In distressed relationships, however, the nurturance pattern is often inadequate and fails to satisfy one or both partners. This is typically due to one or more relationship needs not being met by one or both partners in a satisfying way. Many relationship problems are caused or worsened by frustration and dissatisfaction related to unmet nurturance needs. When either partner believes that the other does not love or care for them in the ways that they desire, it often leads to a significant decline in the frequency and quality of expressed nurturance. This issue is particularly challenging when one partner is unwilling to change the existing pattern.

Couples in distressed relationships often struggle with problems or issues that interfere with their ability to effectively meet their needs for nurturance. A common issue is a nurturance pattern based on conditions, where one or both partners are willing to express love and care only if certain conditions are met first. For example, one partner may agree to sexually intimacy, but only if their own specific needs are met beforehand. In such patterns, love and care are often expressed with the primary goal of fulfilling one's own needs rather than the needs of their partner. This conditional approach can further strain the relationship and reduce overall partner satisfaction.

Another common issue in distressed relationships is the lack of nurturance due to negative emotional reactions. In these situations, attempts to express nurturance are often met with resistance, avoidance, or irritability. One partner may be made to feel ashamed for being perceived as being "needy" or "demanding." This dynamic is frequently associated with shaming, sarcasm, criticism, negativity, or verbal abuse.

For some couples, there may be resistance to change due to one or both partners not openly expressing their specific needs or desires for nurturance. In other cases, one partner may have attempted to express their needs, but these efforts were either ignored or failed to bring about meaningful change. As a result, the unsatisfied partner may lose hope and resign themselves to the belief that their needs will never be met. This often leads to a chronic pattern of dissatisfaction within the relationship or, potentially, the end of the relationship itself. A negative or unsatisfying nurturance pattern is often at the root of many relationship problems and conflicts. Therefore, it is essential for couples to openly discuss their needs and desires to feel loved and cared for. Improving the nurturance pattern is a valuable investment in the long-term health, satisfaction, and success of the relationship.

Improving Intimacy

The first and most important step in developing a healthy pattern of intimacy is for each partner to identify what they need to feel loved and cared for. This step is essential for initiating the process of improving nurturance. Simply discussing each partner's needs is itself an act of care and an important first step toward positive change and growth.

When both partners have a clear understanding of each other's needs and desires, they can create a nurturance plan. This plan identifies the most meaningful ways to express love and care based on each partner's needs. It also defines the type of nurturance desired, how much, and how often it is desired. This provides greater clarity for meeting each partner's needs for nurturance in a way that is most fulfilling to both. This approach reinforces each partner's belief that their relationship is stable and will consistently meet their long-term need to feel loved. Initially, creating a nurturance plan may seem or feel somewhat awkward. Although this process may feel unnatural, it rapidly becomes more comfortable and natural as it quickly leads to significant positive changes and greater satisfaction in the relationship.

Developing a quality nurturance pattern is one of the most valuable investments a person can make in creating a successful long-term relationship. Intimate relationships do not require excessive or unrealistic amounts of nurturance. The time and effort needed to satisfy the needs for nurturance are minimal compared to the significant emotional rewards that come from being in a fulfilling and loving relationship. The path toward achieving the dream of a life-long, satisfying relationship is directly related to the effort invested in creating a satisfying pattern of nurturance, intimacy, and love. Couples who invest time and effort to establishing a mutually fulfilling nurturance pattern will experience greater meaning and satisfaction in their relationships.

In conclusion, nurturance is an essential component of all successful and fulfilling relationships. The ways in which a couple expresses love and nurturance are the most critical factors in building and sustaining relationship wealth. Nurturance forms the foundation of a lasting and deeply satisfying relationship.

6

PLEASURE
ENJOYING LIFE TOGETHER

A need for pleasure exists in all healthy relationships. It is hard to imagine a successful or quality relationship that lacks some degree of pleasure. Many people underestimate the importance of pleasure in their relationship. One of the primary sources of distress in many relationships is a lack of shared activities that provide pleasurable time together.

Pleasure in intimate relationships covers multiple areas of one's life. The need for pleasure encompasses all forms of positive pleasurable experience including sensory pleasure, joy, humor, and play. Pleasurable activities provide emotional gratification, satisfaction, and enjoyment that result from positive experiences, and are an essential component of the Blue Zone.

Pleasure provides several important benefits to a relationship. The primary benefit is that it enriches the bond between partners. Sharing pleasurable activities is an important source of positive feelings that reinforce the bond between intimate partners.

The need for pleasure is an important factor in building relationship wealth. It serves to reinforce the foundation of the relationship, making it more stable and better able to endure stress.

A relationship where mutual pleasure is experienced on a regular basis generally has a greater degree of relationship wealth. These experiences are cumulative and help to reinforce the bond between partners.

Another important benefit of pleasure is that it offsets some of the negative effects of stress. It helps couples to better cope with the many stress factors that are an inevitable part of life and relationships.

Intimate relationships significantly benefit from regular periods of pleasure, fun, playfulness, and joy. The extent and amount of pleasure needed in a relationship is largely determined by the desire of both partners. Each partner's desire for pleasure can vary significantly in terms of the amount and type of activity. Finding a compatible balance of time for pleasurable activities can be a challenge for many couples but is necessary to satisfy the need for pleasure in an intimate relationship.

The ability to play together as a couple is an important factor in creating and enhancing passion in a relationship. Perel (2017) cites the importance of play and novelty to help break the monotony of routine and to reignite passion. Pleasure, in essence, helps to offset the desensitization that occurs in intimate relationships.

Sources of Pleasure

Generally, one of the greatest sources of pleasure in an intimate relationship is nurturance itself. As previously described, expressing and receiving love or nurturance is a primary source of pleasure for most couples. In essence, it feels good to be in a loving and supportive relationship. The interactive nature of pleasure and nurturance is an example of how relationship needs are interconnected and how the satisfaction of one need impacts other relationship needs.

Pleasure can be experienced on several levels including physical, emotional, sensory, and social levels. Each of these levels consist of a diverse range of activities. On a physical level, intimate couples generally find pleasure in sexual intimacy, expressing affection, holding hands, hugs, back rubs, and other forms of physical contact. Just as physical affection plays a major role in nurturance, it also plays a significant role in the shared experience of pleasure as well. Any form of sensual touch contributes to the overall experience of pleasure.

In addition to touch, pleasure can be experienced on other sensory levels as well. For example, seeing one's partner walk into the room, hearing their voice, or getting a scent of their skin can each be a source of sensory pleasure.

Emotional pleasure can also be experienced from a wide range of shared activities. Going out for dinner, watching television, enjoying a movie, going for a walk, and working on home projects are some common activities that are pleasurable for many couples.

On a social level pleasure can be experienced by spending time with family or friends. These and other social activities are helpful in expanding the boundaries of the relationship. Being part of a larger social group in the community can also contribute to a couples' experience of pleasure.

One of the most important sources of pleasure in a relationship is simple communication. Couples who spend time talking and listening to each other tends to feel heard and understood. It can be emotionally satisfying to share ideas, plan together for the future, provide encouragement and support, or express praise, appreciation, and compliments. Pleasure derived from communication strengthens and reinforces the desire to spend time talking with each other. It reinforces the process of working together as a team.

Humor and play are also an important source of pleasure for many couples. Having a sense of humor is often identified by many couples as a significant source of pleasure that has an impact on the quality of their relationship.

The normal everyday problems of life can cause a buildup of stress that can drain a relationship. Pleasure, humor and other sources of joy help to put one's life in perspective by not taking everyday problems more seriously than they need to be. Having a sense of humor frequently helps to minimize stress and can reduce the burden of everyday stress

Pleasure can also be experienced from working together, doing everyday chores and other responsibilities. Many people generally do not think of chores as a source of pleasure. However, there are many couples who enjoy cooking together, working together in the yard, and managing home projects. There is a certain degree of pleasure in working with one's partner to get things done to maintain a quality home together.

The importance of pleasure in intimate relationships can be seen when comparing distressed couples with successful couples. Couples in distressed relationships often complain that their relationship has become routine and boring. One of the reasons for this is that they often spend a small amount of time together in mutually pleasurable activities. As a result, they do not experience the many benefits gained from the pleasure of shared activities.

Whereas successful couples generally share a range of pleasurable activities, distressed couples tend to share few or no pleasurable activities together. Couples that have only a limited number of mutually pleasurable and satisfying activities are generally less satisfied with their relationship overall.

Couples who share few mutually pleasurable activities find that these limited activities begin to feel less enjoyable over time. Even the most pleasurable activities can start to lose some of their appeal over time. Without finding new activities the level of pleasure will inevitably decrease. New pleasurable activities help to replenish the positive energy in a relationship.

Successful relationships generally share multiple sources of pleasure. They participate in a wide range of activities and experiences that provide them with a satisfying level of pleasure. There is a mutual effort to seek out a diverse range of activities to increase the amount of time and number of activities that they can enjoy together. This greater number of shared activities contributes to a greater amount of pleasure and satisfaction in their relationship.

Couples in distressed relationships often focus more on their own individual needs for pleasure than on sharing mutually pleasurable activities. When this imbalance becomes significant or excessive it can be perceived as selfish by the other partner, leaving them feeling dissatisfied, unhappy, and resentful.

Another common characteristic among distressed couples is the competitive nature of their relationship when sharing activities together. There is an emphasis on winning or being better than the other instead of focusing on having fun together. This can quickly take the pleasure out of an activity.

Successful couples strive for a balance of activities that satisfy both relationship needs and their own individual needs. There is an understanding that their needs for pleasure are not identical, and they might encourage each other to participate in activities where there may not be mutual interest. The balance of time spent in these activities is based on fairness. However, priority is generally given to activities that provide mutual pleasure.

A common issue for couples is that one partner may have an interest in an activity that the other partner has little or no interest in. Successful couples try to find ways to share in their partner's interests or to at least be supportive of those interests. They understand the importance of having separate interests and often support each other in these separate interests and activities.

Successful couples frequently have a structured plan of enjoyable activities that they regularly do together. This gives them a positive experience to look forward to and adds predictability to their life. Consequently, they share more positive experiences in a consistent and predictable way. In addition to predictable shared activities successful couples are also open to new or spontaneous activities. This adventurous spirit often creates positive energy that replenishes the positive energy in the relationship.

The strategic approach taken by successful couples is to establish a list or menu of pleasurable activities that allow them to grow as individuals and as a couple. Their success at doing this leads to greater relationship wealth and supports their perception that their relationship is vibrant and alive.

Most people have a fairly good idea of what gives them pleasure. The goal for each couple is to identify those activities that provide pleasure to both partners. Identifying mutually desirable activities that provide pleasure involves creating a pleasure menu. From this menu one can create a structured plan that will satisfy the pleasure needs of each partner and the relationship.

A successful pleasure menu will consist of both regular routine activities and new or spontaneous activities that can be shared together. Trying new activities helps to keep the pleasure menu fresh and avoids desensitization and boredom from becoming a problem that often occurs with recurrent activities. The following example is a sample Pleasure Menu that can serve as a guide for creating a unique menu of activities that focuses on satisfying a couple's specific needs for pleasure.

The Pleasure Menu

Physical intimacy
Going for a walk
Planning a vacation or outing
Going to the movies
Working on a home project
Exercising together
Having dinner together
Travel vacations
Talking about fun or interesting topics
Taking an online class together
Shopping together
Dancing
Giving each other a massage
Getting together with family or friends
Listening to music
Sharing ideas of interest
Develop a hobby together – photography, yoga, cooking, etc.
Exploring new places together

One of the most important activities for couples is to plan a regular date night. There are many creative ways to spend time together. Gottman (2019) suggests a structured plan in which couples deepen their connection through date nights focused on trust, intimacy, and shared goals. This approach is especially helpful when the central focus is on shared experiences of pleasure.

The experience of pleasure is an important need for building relationship wealth. It serves to enhance the overall energy and quality of a relationship. Finding ways to regularly experience pleasure in one's relationship can incrementally support and maintain a successful long-term relationship. The pursuit of pleasure with an intimate partner is a lifelong process that helps to support a quality relationship. As with other relationship needs, having a successful long-term, intimate relationship rests on satisfying the need for pleasure. One of the reasons why successful relationships flourish is because there is a consistent and renewable source of pleasure, joy, and excitement in them. Couples who value their need for shared pleasure are far more effective at building relationship wealth.

7

SECURITY

CREATING A SAFE HARBOR

All healthy relationships are based on a foundation of safety and security. For love to grow within a relationship it is essential that each partner feels secure and confident in their safety. Security rests on the belief that one's relationship is free from threat, harm, injury, or potential loss. Relationships grow and thrive when they are free of anxiety and stress associated with potential threat or harm. Security, therefore, is an essential component of the Blue Zone. Sustaining a long-term quality relationship requires that safety and security in the relationship be assured.

Safety and security are basic primary needs that have their roots in the biology of survival. Our distant ancestors spent much of their time trying to survive multiple threats. Based on Maslow's hierarchy of needs, safety and security rank just above the basic need for food, water and sleep, (Maslow, 2013). Without a secure sense of safety, it is very difficult to sustain love and happiness in a relationship. For genuine love to flourish in an intimate relationship one must feel safe and secure with one's partner. Without security, the health and durability of a quality relationship is unlikely.

Feeling secure with one's partner provides many important benefits to a relationship. The primary benefit is that love, and other positive feelings, will be much more stable and durable. Love and happiness thrive in a secure environment that is free of anxiety and emotional stress. Other important benefits of being in a secure relationship include relationship stability, peace of mind, an increased ability to tolerate stress, freedom to be oneself, greater self-esteem, better communication, a positive attitude, and less overall emotional distress.

All individuals experience some degree of insecurity at times, particularly in a new relationship. However, insecurity can be experienced at any point in a relationship, particularly when there is some perceived threat to the relationship. All couples experience some degree of insecurity at times. This is normal even in the healthiest relationships. The question is not if there will be periods of insecurity, but how well it is managed that will determine its impact on the quality of the relationship.

The Source of Insecurity

Feelings of insecurity are primarily based on fear and anxiety regarding some potential threat to the relationship. The threat can be either an actual threat or an imagined one. Regardless of the type of threat, the effects on the relationship are the same. These include the unpleasant experiences of anxiety, despair, and negative thinking that affect the perceived quality and happiness with the relationship.

Many people bring significant feelings of insecurity into their relationships based on past relationship experiences. Emotional insecurity can originate in early childhood experiences, problems in previous intimate relationships, or experiences in the current relationship.

Early relationship experiences during childhood, beginning with one's attachment to parents set the stage for experiences in later relationships. According to one theory of relationships known as attachment theory, the quality of the parent-child relationship creates the foundation for the way that people relate to others later in life. (Levine and Heller, 2011). Based on these earlier childhood experiences one learns to relate to others in either a secure, anxious, or detached way.

The type of relationship attachment that each individual develops is generally determined by how well childhood needs were met and how secure the childhood environment was. In the case where the parent-child relationship is unpredictable, unsatisfying, or stressful, an anxious or detached style of interaction can develop. Each of these patterns can be much more significant when there is physical trauma or emotional abuse experienced during early childhood. Based on these earlier experiences, an individual's manner of attachment to others will be characterized by feelings of security or insecurity.

Feelings of insecurity can be further intensified during adolescence when negative judgments and criticisms from others start to have a negative impact on one's self-image and self-esteem. It is at this time that one becomes more acutely aware of personal inadequacies or "flaws" regarding appearance, intelligence, athletic ability, and other traits or abilities. For many, a negative and self-critical pattern of thinking may emerge leading to a strong sense of personal inadequacy. This mindset further intensifies and reinforces feelings of security within social relationships.

Another significant source of emotional insecurity can originate from experiences in past romantic relationships. These relationship experiences may have involved personal rejection, physical or emotional abuse, infidelity, or relationship failure. The after effects are often characterized by strong feelings of anxiety, anger, jealousy, and despair. Each of these experiences can have a profound effect on feelings of insecurity in later relationships.

Finally, feelings of insecurity can emerge in one's current relationship. Any issue that is perceived as a potential threat to the stability or durability of one's relationship can lead to feelings of insecurity. Some common examples that can lead to feelings of insecurity are issues related to disloyalty, trust, disrespect, or negative emotional reactions related to conflict. Each of these problems can cause feelings of insecurity that can severely disrupt the stability of a relationship.

Types Of Security

There are generally four types of security that are important in intimate relationships: physical, emotional, social, and financial security. Each of these areas overlaps significantly with the others. While all types of security play an important role in a relationship, emotional security often has the most significant impact.

A healthy and durable relationship requires a solid foundation of security. It is an essential need in all healthy intimate relationships. The stability and satisfaction of each of the other relationship needs is directly affected by how secure each partner feels in the relationship. Love, nurturance, and all the other core relationship needs require security to function in a healthy manner.

Feeling physically secure is probably the most basic level of security in a relationship. This type of security is generally associated with any threat or potential threat to one's physical well-being. It is impossible to have a healthy and secure relationship where the threat of physical harm exists.

In a relationship where there is physical abuse, for example, there is always a threat to one's safety and security. Most people have no tolerance for physical abuse. However, there are many people who become desensitized to abusive behavior and mistakenly believe that it will improve. This is particularly true when the abusive partner is generally stable, supportive, and caring most of the time. Unfortunately, this problem rarely improves without counseling or other intervention. Without feeling physically safe it is not possible to build relationship wealth or to maintain a healthy long-term relationship.

Emotional security is an essential pillar of a quality relationship and is based on the shared belief that each partner values and supports the well-being of the other and strives to maintain the health of the relationship. Additionally, it is also essential that each partner have a shared understanding and assurance that there is a secure level of commitment to the relationship.

Emotional insecurity is often an underlying problem in many relationships and is one of the major causes of distress in relationships. The level of emotional insecurity experienced in a relationship can range from mild to severe. It can be an infrequent issue or can be one that has been an ongoing chronic problem. There can be many indications of insecurity in a relationship. Some of the most frequent are a frequent need for reassurance, over sensitivity to criticism, jealousy, defensiveness, negativity, and a general distrust of others.

Emotional insecurity is often associated with feelings of anxiety, depression, anger, or guilt. These negative feelings are not only unpleasant and stressful but can diminish the level and quality of love and other positive feelings in the relationship. For these reasons it is essential to address feelings of insecurity early on in a relationship.

There are several types of negative behavior that can be a source of emotional insecurity in relationships. This may include verbal abuse, threats of leaving the relationship, false accusations, disloyalty, lying, keeping secrets, withholding affection or physical intimacy, and extreme emotional reactions. Other common sources of emotional insecurity include alcohol or drug abuse, risk-taking behavior, and excessive or inappropriate spending. Any one of these issues can stimulate a significant level of insecurity, anxiety, or other negative feelings, that if not resolved, can put the stability and health of the relationship at risk.

Poor communication can also play a major role in causing emotional insecurity in a relationship. The way in which one partner speaks to the other can lead to misunderstandings, which are often a prime source of emotional insecurity. Negative communication consisting of criticism, negative judgments, sarcasm, hostility, verbal withdrawal, or any negative statement can also be a cause of emotional insecurity. When this pattern is combined with withholding affection or physical intimacy, the effects can become significantly more harmful to the health and durability of the relationship.

Another issue in relationships that can cause feelings of insecurity are competing social relationships. This type of insecurity arises when one partner is seen as being overly involved in other "outside" relationships. The outside relationship is perceived or misperceived as a threat in some way to the integrity of the relationship. These outside relationships can be with family, friends, peers, same sex acquaintances, or even a career or job. Conflicts in this area can be a significant source of anxiety, jealousy, or resentment because of the time or emotional investment involved.

Financial issues are another area of potential insecurity. Many couples struggle with financial issues that affect the security in their relationship. It is one of the leading areas of conflict for many couples. The leading cause of this is a lack of adequate resources to meet needs. Managing finances in a fair and equitable manner is a frequent source of financial insecurity and conflict in many relationships.

It is important to note that there are many couples in successful relationships who lack adequate financial resources yet have a quality relationship. In essence, one can have relationship wealth without financial wealth. On the other hand, there are many couples who are financially well off, but their relationships are emotionally impoverished.

Successful Versus Distressed Relationships

When comparing successful couples with distressed couples there are significant differences regarding security. Predictably, people in challenging relationships often have a greater degree of insecurity and spend much more time struggling with issues related to security needs.

Couples who struggle with deep-seated insecurity more frequently experience emotional stress, conflict, and unhappiness than those in more secure relationships. Significant feelings of insecurity in one or both partners are harmful in two critical ways. The first is the amount of stress that it puts on the relationship. Frequent periods of conflict are almost always harmful to a relationship and often have long term consequences to the health of the relationship.

A second way that insecurity harms relationships is that it disrupts the flow of positive feelings and nurturance within the relationship. Negative emotions associated with insecurity have a toxic effect on the desire to express love, nurturance, and joy. This loss of positive feelings in the relationship reduces the overall quality and resilience needed to maintain relationship wealth.

Distressed couples often react to situations that cause insecurity by avoidance or fighting with each other. This generally leads to further increases in insecurity. As a result, this increased insecurity leads to a further decrease in nurturance, which in turn further increases feelings of insecurity and anxiety, creating a cycle of despair. For this reason, it is essential that couples address feeling of insecurity with care and respect for each other's needs.

Addressing any issue that is a source of insecurity in a relationship can be challenging because there is often significant anxiety and discomfort associated with feelings of insecurity. Many people feel vulnerable when they talk about their feelings of insecurity. The subject is one that is often avoided by many couples. This problem becomes even more challenging when an issue is raised in an accusatory manner. This often leads to denial and defensiveness. For these reasons, it is important to approach issues that cause insecurity carefully and in a supportive manner.

As expected, couples in successful relationships generally and have far less conflict related to insecurity. Within these relationships there is basic trust based on the mutual belief that each partner can depend on the other to respect and support their needs.

Couples in successful relationships are much more responsive to issues or problems that have the potential to cause insecurity within their relationship. They are more protective of their relationship and are careful not to be critical, defensive, or negative toward each other. There also is a greater willingness to find effective ways to reduce feelings of insecurity by directly addressing the source of the insecurity. Consequently, successful couples experience a greater sense of security, experience less stress, and enjoy a greater flow of love and nurturance in their relationship.

Building A Secure Relationship

Healthy relationships clearly require that each partner feel secure within their relationship. To build a more secure relationship requires that a couple identify what each needs to feel secure in their relationship. Security, like trust, is built through the understanding what each partner needs from the other, and then to consistently meet those expectations and needs for security.

As with all relationship needs, the need for security requires open communication where each partner feels that they can freely express what they need to feel secure. As a couple, it is important to take a positive approach toward understanding and acceptance of each other's point of view, allowing each to express their own independent thoughts and feelings. Once there is an understanding of what each partner needs to feel secure then an agreement can be established that will allow them to effectively maintain security in their relationship.

Prevention is a priority when addressing any relationship problem, particularly a problem related to insecurity. By clearly defining what one's needs for security are it is much easier to prevent insecurity before it becomes a much more challenging issue. However, precisely defining these needs can be a challenge because one or both partners may have difficulty expressing their thoughts and feelings in this area, particularly if they feel that their thoughts and feelings could make them feel weak or "needy" in the eyes of the other partner.

The needs and expectations surrounding the issue of security can vary significantly between individuals. At the core of all security needs is the belief and assurance that one's partner will remain committed to the long-term integrity of the relationship. The underlying desire or need is to know that the love and commitment of one's partner will be there in a dependable and consistent way regardless of the challenges of life. Knowing that one has someone to share life with in a loving and meaningful way significantly contributes to one's feelings of security.

Other factors that strengthen security in a relationship include the amount of nurturance expressed, reassurance, a positive attitude about the relationship, dependability, meaningful time spent together, and activities that reinforce the quality of the relationship.

One issue that is often a source of increased security for successful couples, but often a source of significant stress for distressed couples, is the issue of independence and personal space. Everyone has their own specific need for independence and personal space. This varies significantly from individual to individual, and from couple to couple. Sometimes these differences may be seen as a threat in some way to the security of the relationship. This can be a primary source of stress for many couples.

Couples in successful relationships, however, generally see independence and having adequate personal space as a source of greater security, because it allows them to grow as a person separate from their partner. They work together to find a balance between their time with their partner and time spent on personal interests. This is much easier to do when the needs for security and trust are stable.

A healthy relationship is one that consists of interdependence between partners, rather than dependence. Each partner's goals and needs for personal space can benefit the relationship and thereby enhance mutual security. The perception of independence is often seen by couples in successful relationships as a form of nurturance, rather than as a potential threat to the relationship.

A helpful tool to reinforce feelings of security in a relationship is having a security agreement in place that defines the approach to be taken when issues of insecurity arise. This security agreement may include several elements. One such element might be that each partner will have the responsibility to bring up any issue that is a source of insecurity for them and expect that the issue will be treated in a positive, reassuring, and respectful way. It is almost always better to address a problem with insecurity earlier rather than later before it becomes a much larger problem.

Once the cause of insecurity is identified it is important to determine which steps will help resolve or manage the problem. Problems with insecurity, like other significant relationship problems, may require more than one conversation to resolve. This process generally involves an investment of time and energy, but the effort can prevent the problem from escalating or continuing in the future. The investment made in this process is a powerful form of caring that helps to reinforce the feelings of security in the relationship.

One of the most important tools that can be used to both reduce insecurity and to significantly improve feelings of security are intermittent doses of reassurance when needed. The consistent use of reassurance is an important medicine in healing the underlying anxiety associated with insecurity. In fact, reassurance is a powerful tool and a significant form of nurturance that instills confidence and security in a relationship.

There will be times when the problem of insecurity is so entrenched that it may be extremely difficult to resolve. This can be a significant source of emotional distress within the relationship. In these situations, it may be best to seek counseling to address the underlying issues responsible for the problem. Frequently, these problems stem from earlier experiences that have little or nothing to do with the current relationship.

Factors that Increase Security

- Early recognition of the problem
- Open communication
- Positive approach
- Acceptance
- Supportive environment
- Prevention
- Reassurance
- Strategic agreement

- Implementation
- Independent growth / Individuality
- Maintenance

Building a stable level of security in a relationship should always be a priority. Improving security is a gradual and continuous process that requires time and effort from both partners. The foundation of a healthy relationship rests on the essential need for security. Building and maintaining a stable and durable level of security is essential for establishing a successful long-term relationship. Feeling safe and secure in a relationship helps each partner to grow and become the best version of oneself. Building security in a relationship can be achieved by any couple with the desire to work together to achieve this goal. It requires an attitude that conveys a desire to make security in one's relationship a priority. Ultimately, the time and effort invested in this area contributes to building relationship wealth and allows one to enjoy the many benefits of being in a lifelong quality relationship.

THE GREEN ZONE

8

SHARED LEADERSHIP

IT TAKES TWO!

One of the most important qualities of successful relationships is leadership. The ability to work effectively with one's partner in meeting each other's needs will be a major factor in determining the quality and longevity of a relationship. Good leadership is not only important for building a healthy relationship but is important to ensure the long-term stability of the relationship. It allows a relationship to grow stronger, remain stable, and provide a higher degree of emotional satisfaction. Leadership is involved in all aspects of a relationship, including one's attitude, thinking, communication, and the way one interacts with a partner. Finally, effective leadership provides a protective barrier that shields the relationship from stress.

Leadership helps to build a quality relationship by opening channels of communication, identifying the important needs of the relationship, and creating a plan to successfully meet those needs. In many respects, leadership is an important component of the Green Zone. Without effective leadership a relationship is vulnerable to the effects of emotional stress to a much greater degree.

Leadership can be defined as the ability to successfully direct or lead oneself from where one is to where one needs to be. Leadership in a relationship requires that there be an understanding of what the needs are, and where one would like the relationship to be in terms of quality and stability. To achieve this involves understanding each partner's needs, how to meet those needs, and establishing a consistent approach to effectively meet those needs.

The primary function of leadership is to help build and maintain a quality relationship that meets needs, provides positive emotional experiences, and maintains long term stability in a relationship. In essence, leadership helps to guide or direct one's communication and behavior toward the goal of successfully meeting the needs of the relationship.

There are several important benefits that leadership provides to a relationship. The first is that it provides a structure or process by which to manage the everyday business of solving problems, making decisions, meeting needs, and managing stress. This allows for a greater level of stability, resolves conflicts, reduces stress, and increases emotional satisfaction.

Another characteristic of effective leadership is that the approach taken in managing problems and conflicts emphasizes a positive perspective based on respect and tolerance of stress. There is a priority placed on providing support for each other's viewpoint, suggestions, and opinions.

Couples in successful relationships generally believe that their relationship will be a successful and that their relationship needs will be satisfied. They are confident in their ability to satisfy each other's needs and feel secure in their belief that they will be able to work out their problems together.

Couples in distressed relationships, on the other hand, often have negative expectations about being able to work out their problems successfully. They often are resistant to suggestions or influence from their partner and frequently focus more on weaknesses and differences than on areas of agreement. This negative focus often leads to significantly more stress, which in time can take a toll on the relationship.

Effective leadership also provides a protective dimension to a relationship. It allows one to maintain the health of the relationship by managing potential problems before they become a source of conflict or stress. Problems and conflicts have the potential to negatively impact or weaken one's relationship, so it is important to have strategies that will help to manage these problems as they arise. Effective leadership provides for better management of conflict, which helps to prevent stress from eroding the quality of the relationship.

Types of Leadership

Many problems and conflicts in relationships occur because of leadership problems. Poor or ineffective leadership is often a significant factor in failed relationships. Generally, there are at least three primary patterns of leadership commonly seen in intimate relationships. These include a dominance pattern, an avoidance pattern, and a co-leadership pattern. However, there are many variations within these leadership patterns.

One of the most common leadership patterns seen in relationships is one in which one or both partners attempt to dominate or control the relationship decision-making process. When both partners seek dominance over the other, conflict often ensues. This frequently results in a power struggle in which each partner seeks to control the decisions made in their relationship. This can lead to a chronic pattern of conflict between couples as to who will have final say in making decisions in the relationship. In these cases, each person attempts to get their way with little or no desire for compromise. These relationships are often characterized by frequent power struggles. Consequently, each partner becomes increasingly angry, frustrated, and unhappy with the other, and the relationship begins to weaken.

In other relationships, one partner may be dominant, while the other partner tends to be submissive or compliant. When this pattern is acceptable to both partners couples are generally able to establish a functional relationship that is tolerable to both. However, in many of these relationships there is underlying resentment and dissatisfaction that impedes the level of satisfaction that they might otherwise have.

In those cases where one partner wants to have an equal voice or role in decision-making, and the other partner wants to make most or all the relationship decisions, conflicts often arise. There may be displays of dominance, emotional withdrawal, hostility, criticism, and even aggressive behavior. This pattern often results in a significant increase in resentment, frustration, and unhappiness in the "passive" partner. The dominance pattern often has its roots in past relationship experiences in which getting one's way was accomplished using aggressive communication and controlling behavior. This pattern often is based on the belief that the best way to get one's needs met is by controlling the decision-making process.

Another leadership pattern is one of avoidance. In an avoidance pattern there is either no leadership or an inadequate level of leadership, particularly when addressing relationship problems and conflicts. As a result, problems are not adequately resolved, relationship needs are not met, and stress on the relationship is significantly greater. These conditions make it extremely difficult to build and maintain the quality and stability of the relationship.

The avoidance pattern of leadership is often based on anxiety and a belief that making decisions will lead to some negative outcome. One such fear is that it will cause conflict with one's partner, which will lead to unpleasant emotional consequences. It is a pattern where it is easier to avoid problems than tolerate the potential negative consequences of making a mistake or being wrong. Individuals that are frequently criticized for the decisions that they make are likely to fall into an avoidance pattern.

Another common factor contributing to the development of an avoidance pattern is when one or both partners have a history of being in relationships in which they were dependent on others to meet their needs. This past pattern of dependency is often recreated in a new relationship. In some cases, these individuals believe that when their partner makes decisions for them it is an act of love and caring for them.

Generally, both the dominance and avoidance patterns of leadership can have serious consequences for the health, satisfaction, and longevity of a relationship. Each is significantly limited in effectively meeting the needs of the relationship, are less satisfying, and often create significant emotional stress on the relationship. Depending on the overall stress load on the relationship, the long-term durability and quality of the relationship is likely to be much more limited, and the probability of relationship failure is greater.

Self-leadership

Great leadership in a relationship begins with effective self-leadership. Building a successful relationship requires that each partner be responsible for addressing their own personal needs, instead of relying on their partner to fulfill them. When each partner assumes responsibility for their own needs, it reduces the work load on one's partner, which in turn reduces stress on the relationship. Successful relationships, in essence, involve effectively taking care of one's own personal needs, the needs of the relationship, and providing support to one's partner in meeting their personal needs.

Effective self-leadership consists of being able to express what one needs to feel satisfied and content in the relationship. One partner should not be expected to automatically know and understand the needs of the other partner. It is each partner's responsibility to express and manage their own needs, feelings, and behaviors, particularly those actions that impact the relationship. Successful self-leadership is directly related to how well one manages leadership responsibilities in the relationship. If each partner is effective at managing and meeting their own needs, then they will be much better able to share relationship leadership responsibilities with their partner.

Co-leadership

The pattern of leadership most often found in successful relationships is one that is based on the co-leadership model. This model proposes that the success of building and maintaining a quality relationship is directly related to a couple's ability to effectively share leadership responsibilities. Co-leadership involves the ability to lead, communicate needs and ideas, share decision making, compromise, and successfully implement agreements. Each of these abilities plays a significant role in how successful a couple will be in meeting the needs of their relationship.

Healthy co-leadership involves both partners having a voice in relationship decision-making. Real (2007) writes that quality relationships involve empowering both partners without one partner dominating or providing caretaking. In essence, there needs to be a balance so that both partners can thrive together.

Co-leadership requires that both partners work together as a team to meet the needs of the relationship. Co-leadership works best when both partners actively share in the decision-making process. However, co-leadership does not necessarily mean that leadership responsibilities are equally shared. When one partner has a higher level of knowledge or skill in a specific area, it makes sense for them to assume a leadership role in addressing the need.

Co-leadership requires a certain degree of flexibility in terms of addressing problems and needs in a relationship. It is important to know when to lead independently, when to share leadership, and when to follow the lead of one's partner. However, regardless of which partner takes leadership responsibility on an issue it is essential that each partner have a voice in the decision-making process.

The co-leadership model is based on the idea that both partners can freely contribute their thoughts and ideas in the decision-making process. Open communication is necessary in working together to define, negotiate, and compromise on issues that are important to meet the needs of the relationship. The probability of solving relationship problems and meeting needs successfully is much greater when both partners feel that they have played a role in the process.

Sharing leadership and accepting direction from others is difficult for many people. This is often a source of conflict that can lead to one partner becoming oppositional and resistant to suggestions from the other. However, when one partner is open to shared leadership and can accept the influence of the other partner, they are much more likely to be able to sustain a healthy and durable relationship.

The ability to share leadership in a relationship depends on several factors. Leadership does not consist of just one factor but is made up of several components. These include having a shared vision, an effective relationship plan, and a clear mission to meet the needs of a relationship.

A Shared Vision

An important quality in relationship leadership is a shared vision. This vision, in essence, is the mutual view that each partner shares regarding what a successful relationship should look like. It essentially unifies a compatible view of a successful relationship. Having a shared vision provides clarity and stability to a relationship. It serves as a compass or roadmap that provides a positive and meaningful direction for the growth and development of the relationship.

Most couples have different views as to what makes a relationship successful. Fortunately, it is not necessary for each partner to have the same exact vision to have a successful relationship. However, it is important to have a clear understanding of the major points of agreement so that there is a shared vision of the future together. A vision that represents the dreams of each partner and that provides a clear plan as to how to meet those needs enables a couple to successfully build and maintain a successful long-term relationship.

A common problem for many couples is that one partner assumes that the other partner shares the same vision or definition of what a quality relationship consists of. It is frequently assumed that both partners have a compatible vision of the relationship. This belief is often the source of problems that develop later in the relationship. For example, one partner may have a vision in which they will be involved in any decision regarding spending money. However, the other partner may have the idea that they should be able to make any purchase without first discussing it with their partner. A shared vision essentially outlines important areas or points of agreement so that future misunderstandings can be avoided.

The Relationship Plan

Leadership in quality relationships often involves having a clearly defined relationship plan. This plan outlines the needs that each partner believes are most important to having a successful relationship. By understanding each other's needs, it is easier to create an effective relationship plan to meet those needs. The future success of a relationship will depend largely on having an effective plan, and being able to implement the plan to meet relationship needs.

A successful relationship plan clearly defines what, when, and how specific relationship needs are met. However, this does not mean that a couple should establish some rigid or restrictive approach or plan. Instead, having a flexible plan simply clarifies the importance of each partner's needs so that there is greater clarity in meeting those needs. This creates a more consistent way of meeting needs and prevents misunderstandings that lead to the frustration associated with unsatisfied needs. A relationship where partners' needs are consistently satisfied is one with a greater degree of quality, stability, and durability.

An effective relationship plan is an investment of communication and time. However, without a plan there is an increased probability that far more time will be spent feeling dissatisfied with the relationship. A good relationship plan, in essence, serves as a maintenance plan. Just as it is necessary to maintain one's health, car, or house, it is important to have a plan to maintain the health of a relationship so that it remains stable, durable, and emotionally satisfying.

Maintaining a quality relationship requires the ability to adapt to life changes and needs. An effective relationship plan therefore needs to be flexible to adapt to the changing needs of the relationship. Just as one's individual needs change over time, so do the needs of one's relationship change. For this reason, it is important to periodically review the needs of one's relationship so that relationship needs are being met, and to prevent emotional dissatisfaction.

Over time, a relationship will face many challenges, each of which will require different skills, knowledge, and experience. Some of the more significant challenges may include issues related to raising children, finances, health, work schedules, and many of the other everyday issues that couples must manage. The ability to negotiate these challenges in a balanced and fair manner is essential to the long-term success of a relationship.

The Mission

Leadership in successful relationships depends on having a clearly defined mission or purpose. The primary mission of an intimate relationship consists of two major parts. The first part of the mission is to successfully enrich and maintain a quality relationship by consistently satisfying the needs of the relationship. This requires that there be agreement as to what is needed to effectively nurture and support the long-term health and stability of the relationship.

The second part of the relationship mission is to protect the relationship from those factors that can weaken or diminish the health or quality of the relationship. In any relationship there will be many challenging problems that can cause significant emotional stress. These problems and challenges have the potential to weaken or diminish the quality of a relationship. Protecting one's relationship from the effects of problems and emotional stress is critically important to prevent the relationship from harm that can lead to relationship failure. The mission or goal should be to prevent problems from developing when possible, resolving problems in a timely manner, and regulating emotions so that any potential harm to the relationship is minimized.

Building and maintaining a successful relationship does not happen by accident. Successful couples have a deliberate leadership plan that provides an effective approach for meeting the needs of their relationship. This is accomplished through the fair sharing of leadership responsibilities so the needs of the relationship can be effectively met. Successful co-leadership is based on a mutually created vision, plan of action, and a clear mission. The major purpose of relationship co-leadership is to serve as a roadmap for building and maintaining a quality long-term relationship.

9

COMMUNICATION

BUILDING A BRIDGE TO EACH OTHER

Communication is one of the most important needs in intimate relationships. Without communication it is impossible to bond and form relationships with others. Communication and relationship success is directly linked to each other, with changes in one directly affecting the other. Establishing and maintaining a successful and durable relationship requires that couples communicate effectively with each other. The quality and stability of a relationship is directly related to the quality of the communication between partners.

Communication is essential for meeting all the other needs in a relationship. Expressions of love, solving problems, meeting needs, and mutual understanding all require effective communication. For example, communication is necessary for meeting the needs in the Blue Zone, including the expression of love and nurturance, sharing pleasure, and to address issues related to security. Communication is also needed to meet the needs in the Green Zone, to solve problems in the Yellow Zone, and to prevent and manage emotional stress in the Red Zone. Communication, therefore, is an essential tool that is necessary to increase relationship wealth and build a strong and healthy relationship.

Communication is the essence of all human relationships. In his excellent book on communication, Rosenberg (2015) writes that the way we communicate with others and with ourselves ultimately determines the quality of our lives. This is particularly true for our most intimate relationships.

Communication is defined herein as the verbal and nonverbal flow of information between partners for the purpose of meeting needs. It consists of everything that one says or does when interacting with a partner. Verbal communication is expressed with words, while nonverbal communication consists of facial expressions, eye contact, tone of voice, and gestures. Although communication consists of what one says and does, it can also include what is not said or done. For example, if one partner says to the other, "I love you," and the other partner remains silent then, in essence, the silence is communicating a message.

Successfully meeting relationship needs depends largely on effective communication. On a basic level communication is generally effective in meeting relationship needs. However, in many situations, communication can be limited, ineffective, and inadequate. People often assume that when they express themselves verbally that their words are clearly and accurately understood by the other person. Unfortunately, this assumption is frequently not the case. Consequently, misunderstandings are common, which often leads to conflict and relationship dissatisfaction. Understanding the weaknesses and limitations of communication can help partners to avoid misunderstandings that cause many problems in relationships.

The primary purpose of communication is sharing information, meeting needs, expressing feelings, and sharing affection and intimacy. Successful couples understand the importance of communication in meeting their needs and having a quality relationship. They are also generally more aware of the limitations of communication and are ready to seek clarity about an issue that might be a problem.

The Benefits of Quality Communication

There are a many important benefits of effective communication. One of the most important benefits is that it leads to a greater understanding of what each partner needs in a relationship. Couples in successful relationships learn to develop the ability to express themselves clearly, and to listen to each other in a focused and attentive way. This pattern of understanding improves their ability to identify and more effectively meet the needs of their relationship. Good communication also improves their ability to identify and prevent problems early in the relationship. This allows them to address problems in a timelier manner, which reduces stress on the relationship.

Another major benefit of being able to communicate effectively is that it increases emotional closeness between partners. As a result, emotional intimacy and relationship wealth increase in the relationship. The multiple benefits that effective communication provides play a major role in building and maintaining a strong and durable intimate relationship. Learning to improve communication, therefore, is an important investment that can lead to a dramatic improvement in the quality of one's relationship.

Communication consists of two major components, speaking and listening. These two factors together form a communication cycle consisting of expressive communication (Speaking), and receptive communication (Listening). Each one of these components is critical in the process of understanding and meeting the needs of a relationship. Communication generally flows in a cycle. One partner thinks of something that they want to say, they express it to their partner, the other partner listens, thinks about it, and then responds back, and so forth. This process of talking and listening continues in a cyclical fashion until an understanding between the partners is achieved.

Effective communication is a dynamic process that attempts to build a clear understanding of what each partner needs from the other. Initially, there may be little or no understanding of a subject that is brought up. As the communication process continues, understanding increases to the point where both partners believe they understand each other. In a sense, it is like building an understanding by using communication as a tool and words are the bricks used to construct the understanding.

One way to think about communication is to imagine a communication bridge connecting one partner to the other. As partners talk and listen to each other, information passes back and forth across this bridge. This information travels along two tracks from one partner to the other. One track is a verbal or information track that consists primarily of words that convey the content or message that one partner wants to send to the other. The other track is the emotional track, which carries the emotional meaning associated with the words. The emotional track consists largely of nonverbal communication such as tone of voice, facial expressions, and gestures. The emotional track generally conveys feelings, interest level, perceived importance of a subject, attitude, respect, and other important information. For example, one might use words to say, "Good morning." However, on the emotional track the tone of voice can be either upbeat and positive, or it could be sarcastic. In essence, the verbal track consists of what is said, and the emotional track is how it is said.

Expressive Communication

The ability to express oneself effectively is essential to having a quality long-term relationship. It is important that couples be able to clearly express their needs, thoughts, and feelings in a way that allows their partner to understand them. In many ways, this process is relatively easy and straightforward. However, communication problems can easily develop due to basic misunderstandings.

As mentioned above, the ability to express oneself clearly is based not only on what is said, but also how it is said. How one partner talks to the other can frequently be more predictive of the success of a relationship than the content of the message alone. The way that individuals express themselves through their attitude, tone of voice, and facial expression can have a significant impact on how effective communication will be. Nonverbal communication is often a primary source of misunderstandings in relationships. For example, using a hostile or loud tone of voice, rolling the eyes, frowning, and finger pointing are all examples of negative communication that can not only reduce the quality of communication but can also be toxic to the relationship.

Unfortunately, communication is frequently used in a harmful or destructive way. Couples in distressed relationships often express words in a negative way without realizing that they can cause long-term damage to their relationship. Even worse, they sometimes use words as weapons to criticize, devalue, belittle, shame, or hurt. This negative communication is often a part of verbal or emotional abuse that can lead to significant harm to the long-term stability of a relationship. This type of harm frequently radiates well into the future and can often be permanent. For this reason, prevention is an essential factor in protecting one's relationship from this destructive pattern of communication.

Common Problems in Communication

Poor communication is one of the most common problems cited by couples in struggling relationships. It is also one of the leading causes of relationship failure. One of the primary reasons for this is that communication has many limitations and pitfalls. A common communication problem is a misunderstanding where words, intentions, feelings, and needs are not accurately perceived or understood by one or both partners. This type of misunderstanding can lead to significant emotional stress and conflict, which then places a heavy burden on the relationship.

There are several causes of misunderstandings in communication. One significant problem is that words may be limited in their ability to accurately convey the meaning intended. Words can be vague and unclear, or even have multiple meanings. As a result, it is easy to misinterpret what is being said. The greater the clarity of the words used the better the communication will be.

A second major problem that can lead to misunderstandings is the impact of emotions. The more emotional a subject is, the greater the potential for a misunderstanding to occur. When one or both partners are experiencing a high-level of emotion, distortions in listening and thinking tend to be greater, which makes it more likely for misunderstandings to occur. This is why having control over one's emotions is essential to maintaining stability in a relationship.

Another cause of misunderstandings is the lack of adequate communication. Some partners share very little or provide only limited explanations of what they mean. As result, it is more challenging to accurately understand or interpret what they think and feel about any given issue. Additionally, people often express themselves based on the mistaken assumption that the person to whom they are speaking clearly understands exactly what they mean. The reality is that this is often not true. For these reasons, when expressing thoughts, feelings, or needs, it is important to confirm that one's partner clearly understands what has been said. This will help to prevent misunderstandings that can lead to unnecessary stress on the relationship.

Communication in Successful Relationships

Couples in successful relationships communicate with each other using an effective approach that reinforces and strengthens the core needs in their relationship. This process begins with a positive attitude or mindset and is based on the belief that every communication and interaction between partners is an opportunity to strengthen their bond together and to build relationship wealth.

Couples in successful relationships use much more positive communication to build, develop, and maintain their relationships. They more frequently use positive words and language in their conversations, particularly when describing each other. Additionally, they are more complimentary, more encouraging, and more frequently express appreciation for each other.

Their nonverbal communication is also more positive including their tone of voice, facial expressions, and gestures. They smile more, nod more to show understanding or agreement, maintain better eye contact, and use touch frequently to connect with each other.

The consistent use of positive communication effectively builds and maintains the strength and durability of successful relationships. Positive communication including expressions of love, kindness, support, and encouragement are at the heart of building relationship wealth and form the backbone of successful relationships.

Successful couples also have a much more secure pattern of communication, particularly when there is disagreement or conflict. Freedom of speech is encouraged so that any subject can be openly discussed. They can speak their minds and express thoughts and feelings openly without concern for negative responses from each other. Because of this degree of comfort, they can have deeper and more meaningful conversations.

When observing successful couples interacting with each other, it generally appears that they have a fondness and respect for each other. There are many ways in which positive communication is expressed in their relationship. It is not just what is said but how it is said that makes a significant difference between successful and distressed couples. Successful couples are much more consistently positive in their communication with each other. The following examples consist of many of the positive qualities that are essential to building and maintaining a quality long-term relationship.

Improving Expressive Communication

- Create a positive mindset or attitude
- Begin conversations with a positive statement
- Maintain a consistent positive focus using positive words and statements
- Positive nonverbal expressions - tone of voice, eye contact, facial expressions, and touch
- Emotional expression – Ability to express both positive and negative feelings

- Able to speak openly and honestly about ideas, feelings, and needs
- Respect – Use of words that indicate respect for partner's feelings, ideas, and needs
- Express approval and acceptance of partner
- Make encouraging statements
- Recognize positive qualities or achievements.
- Show appreciation for the things that their partner does
- Compliment partners
- Humor – Able to use humor when appropriate
- Assertive – Able to ask for what they want and need directly
- Encouragement – make encouraging statements to support and empower their partner
- Team Focus – More frequent use of the word "We" versus "I"
- Ask questions to build understanding of relationship needs
- Focus on one issue at a time

Communication in Distressed Relationships

Couples in distressed relationships, on the other hand, are much more likely to focus communication on the negative aspects of their relationship. They express more negative words and statements, often using sarcasm, hostility, and criticism. Their nonverbal communication generally suggests a lack of interest, irritability, anger, or a certain degree of contempt or dislike for what the other partner says. Such partners also tend to be more oppositional, defensive, resistant to change, and demanding. They often talk more about themselves and their needs instead of focusing on their partner's needs. Their overall communication is characterized by disdain and a lack of respect for their partner's opinions and feelings.

People in distressed relationships often do not feel able to speak freely about problems and issues that trouble them. As a result, they will often avoid speaking openly and directly about problems, and instead will express their feelings through a negative attitude or behavior which often leads to more frequent misunderstandings, which then contributes to further conflict and unhappiness.

Intentional Listening

Effective listening is the other critical component of communication. Successful relationships are based on effective communication; and successful communication is based on effective listening. Listening is not passive or just reactive. It is more than simply hearing and involves a deeper level of understanding. Listening sometimes requires much more work than speaking. As a result, a much more conscious effort and determined attitude is required to develop this skill effectively.

Listening is such an essential component of communication that in some ways it is even more important than speaking. The primary purpose of listening in intimate relationships is to gain a clear understanding of what each partner's needs are. To achieve this understanding requires the ability to effectively listen in a very focused way without being distracted by one's thoughts. Frequently, there is a tendency to pay more attention to what one wants to say, rather than truly listening to fully understand what the other person is saying. This imbalance in communication is responsible for many misunderstandings that are the cause of many of the communication problems found in distressed relationships.

There can be no genuine understanding without effective listening. Understanding the needs of one's partner depends much more on listening than talking. To achieve a quality and stable relationship it is essential to listen in an intentional and focused way, to understand what one's partner needs, what they like and dislike, what motivates them, and most importantly, what they need to feel secure and loved.

It is important to note that listening is clearly different from simply hearing. Hearing is an acknowledgement that one has heard what the other person has said. Listening on the other hand is intentional and focused. There is a clear focus on the attention to the speaker's message or point, what they are feeling, and what they need or desire.

Intentional listening leads to a greater level of clarity and understanding of what each partner wants or desires from the other. For example, do they have a question? Do they want to vent their feelings? Do they have a problem that they want help them with? Or do they have some need that they are trying to meet?

The Benefits of Listening

Listening provides several important benefits to a healthy and successful relationship. The most important benefit is that it provides an understanding of what each partner needs to feel happy and satisfied in the relationship.

Although listening can serve the purpose of receiving information, it can also be a form of expression. In essence, listening is a form of caring that shows interest and value in what the other person says and reinforces positive feelings and emotional closeness in the relationship. On a deeper level listening may be viewed not only as a form of caring, but also as an expression of love. In fact, listening can express love just as powerfully as speaking. On the other hand, a lack of listening can express a negative message that suggests a lack of caring or value in the other person's ideas, feelings, or needs.

Another benefit of listening is that it helps to reduce stress by allowing one's partner to express or vent emotions and stress. Many issues and problems in relationships are associated with anxiety, frustration, and other emotions. Listening serves as an outlet for these feelings which helps to reduce emotional distress and maintain relationship stability.

Another significant benefit of focused listening is that it increases the willingness of the one's partner to listen. When one partner can fully express their point of view, they are likely to be more open to fully listening in return. There is also a greater likelihood that one's ideas and feelings will be giving greater thought and consideration.

Listening obviously provides many benefits that provide support to a quality relationship. Many of these benefits are essential to the long-term stability and health of a successful relationship. Developing effective listening skills is a critical skill that will provide numerous benefits over the course of a relationship.

Benefits Summary

- Improves the understanding of relationship needs
- Conveys interest, approval, and acceptance
- Expresses love and nurturance
- Increases emotional closeness
- Encourages the expression of ideas and feelings
- Reduces stress
- Increases relationship stability
- Encourages listening in return

Common Problems in Listening

One of the most frequent complaints that people have in their relationships is that their partner doesn't listen to them. This is particularly true in distressed relationships. Although communication in general is one of the most significant factors in failed relationships, poor listening is the primary reason for many communication problems.

Getting one's partner to listen begins with our own ability to listen effectively. Our listening with empathy sets the stage for our partner to listen better. People are more likely to be willing to listen when they feel heard (Sofer, 2018).

The lack of adequate listening frequently causes couples to draw premature conclusions. This problem is often a primary source of conflict in relationships since misunderstandings are a major source of stress on relationships.

Listening can be extremely challenging for many people. One of the problems in listening is the ability to maintain attention for an extended period. The process of listening requires that one be able to concentrate on what is being said, accurately interpret its meaning or importance, manage one's emotional reaction, identify the need and, finally, respond back in a way that indicates understanding and empathy.

Many people are marginal listeners at best. As mentioned earlier, one of the major reasons for this is because listening takes a lot more work and concentration than the effort needed for talking. It takes time, patience, and the ability to maintain concentration when listening. Many people have a short attention span that causes them to become easily distracted, especially when they find the subject to be of little or no importance. When you compare the work and complexity of listening with that of talking it is easy to see why people prefer talking to listening. It has been said that the reason that we have only one mouth, but two ears, is so that we can listen twice as much as we speak.

Effective listening depends on listening fully without interruption. The inability to listen without interruption is another frequent problem in relationships. Many people prefer to talk about their own point of view on any given subject. They are more interested in expressing their own thoughts and feelings rather than listening to what the other person has to say. Even when listening they are often focusing on what their response will be rather than fully listening to what the other person is saying.

Interruptions are another impediment to good communication. One of the reasons for this is based on the belief that listening implies agreement. This idea, especially during disagreements, frequently leads to interruptions. Many people think that if they remain silent, it implies that they agree with what is being said. As a result, they will interrupt to make the point that they disagree with a particular idea or point.

Interruptions, in essence, can dramatically reduce the overall quality of the communication. To avoid this, it is important to listen until one's partner is finished expressing their viewpoint. One of the major benefits of fully listening in a focused way is that much of the meaning of what a person says is often at the back end of the statement. As a result, interrupting the speaker before they have finished can dramatically reduce the level of understanding. Avoiding interruptions therefore helps to improve the overall level of understanding.

Generally, one of the most difficult times to listen effectively is when one is emotionally distressed. Generally, the more emotionally charged or intense a subject is, the greater the probability that the communication will suffer, and misunderstandings will arise. Once the emotional stress level reaches a certain threshold, the ability to listen effectively becomes impaired.

Primary Listening Problems

- Misunderstanding of needs
- Drawing premature conclusions
- Interruptions
- Focusing on one's response instead of listening
- Emotional factors
- Silence or a lack of speaking
- Negative reactions in partner

Listening in Successful Relationships

Generally, it may not always be easy to see clear differences in communication between couples in successful relationships and those in distressed relationships, particularly when talking about emotionally neutral subjects. However, when it comes to listening there are some clear differences. The primary difference is that couples in distressed relationships generally do not listen well. They often listen to only fragments of what their partner says. Consequently, they often miss important information necessary to fully understanding each other.

Communication is an essential tool by which successful couples build relationship wealth and establish long-term quality relationships. The importance of effective listening is one of the hallmarks of couples in successful relationships. They generally realize that listening is one of the most important forms of caring. Few things say that one cares more than listening to what matters to one's partner.

As a skill, listening can be learned and improved to dramatically improve communication. It does, however, require deliberate practice to develop this skill. There are several ways in which listening can be improved. One strategy is to simply practice using intentional listening to better understand the meaning of what one's partner says. This type of listening intentionally seeks information in the listening process to gain a clear understanding of what their partner is communicating. In essence, successful couples have a purpose and focused approach to listening that leads to a greater level of clarity in their communication.

Intentional listening leads to a clearer understanding of what each partner needs, and how to meet those needs more effectively. For example, does one partner have a particular need that they are trying to meet? Do they have a problem that they want to discuss? Or do they want to connect in a nurturing way? Intentional listening helps to more quickly identify the need so that it can be addressed more effectively.

Intentional listening involves being able to put one's_thoughts aside to concentrate on the words and feelings that one's partner is trying to express. It is natural to have thoughts and feelings while listening. However, the goal of intentional listening is to maintain a focus on one's partner at the same time. This is one of the primary reasons why listening is so much more difficult than speaking. Successful couples learn to become effective at doing this and can delay expressing their thoughts and feelings until they fully understand their partner's thoughts and feelings.

An effective and helpful way to improve intentional listening is by using the acronym SEND. The S represents the subject or point being expressed by one's partner. The E represents the emotion or feeling that is being expressed. The emotion expressed often conveys how important the issue is to the person speaking. The N represents the need that underlies the subject of what is being said. Finally, the letter D represents what to do in response to what the other person is saying or asking. Frequently, the first and most important thing to do is to continue listening; or if the person is done speaking, to ask questions that will lead to greater clarity and understanding of what they need. This approach to listening helps partners listen on multiple levels of understanding instead of just listening to words.

An important skill that couples in successful relationships learn to develop is the ability to listen when one or both partners are emotionally distressed. They are better able to regulate and manage their feelings and emotions to avoid an escalation of the conflict. Listening becomes much more challenging when talking about an emotionally stressful problem because these feelings can disrupt the ability to listen effectively. Emotions tend to cause the rate or flow of communication to increase. This frequently leads to an increase in misunderstandings, which then further intensify emotions and conflict. Intentional listening functions to slow down the rate of communication so that emotions can be more easily controlled or managed.

Another important difference is that when there is conflict, successful couples generally listen for points that they can agree upon first. This allows each partner to feel heard and respected. Once this pattern of cooperation is established, they are in a much better position to address the points of disagreement.

Learning to improve the ability to listen more effectively is one of the best possible investments that one can make in a relationship. With consistent practice, listening can dramatically improve the quality and effectiveness of communication. Although this skill can be difficult to achieve consistently, it can rapidly improve with practice. An effective strategy for partners is to start by giving complete and undivided attention, without interruption, to at least one conversation each day, then gradually working toward the goal of consistently listening at this level during every conversation.

How to Improve Intentional Listening

- Listen intentionally
- Identify the key idea or need that the other partner is trying to convey
- Use the acronym SEND (Subject, Emotion, Need, Do)
- Listen, ask questions, and continue to listen
- Listen with patience
- Maintain eye contact
- Acknowledge each point
- Focus on what is said rather than on own thoughts
- Avoid interruptions
- Stay focused in the present moment
- Respond to all communication attempts
- Pay attention to both words and behavior to improve understanding
- Identify the points of agreement first before points of disagreement
- Empathy – Imagine what it might be like in the other partner's situation
- Slow the rate of speaking as emotions increase.

In conclusion, quality communication is a powerful tool in building and sustaining successful relationships. Effective communication is not only the exchange of words but, more importantly, understanding the emotions and needs underlying those words. The investment of time and effort toward improving communication, both speaking and listening, will substantially enhance relationship satisfaction and stability. The improvement in this skill will lead to a positive cycle of mutual understanding, respect, and love. This process significantly increases relationship wealth and provides the foundation for a quality long-term relationship.

10

TRUST

COUNTING ON EACH OTHER

The importance of trust in intimate relationships is well established. All healthy relationships depend on a solid foundation of trust. In fact, without trust it wouldn't be possible to have the level of relationship wealth necessary for a healthy long-term relationship.

But what exactly is trust? One definition is that trust is the belief that one can rely on the character, integrity, and honesty of another person. In the case of an intimate relationship, trust is based on the beliefs, feelings, and experiences one has in a relationship with a partner. It is an understanding or conviction based on the belief and confidence that one can depend on a partner to support the best interests and well-being of the relationship.

The need for trust is essential to all healthy relationships because it is directly related and connected to the need for safety and emotional security. Trust, therefore, is an essential component of the Green Zone. Building and maintaining trust is essential to the health, stability, and longevity of any intimate relationship.

The Benefits of Trust

The ability to completely trust one's partner in a close and personal relationship provides several important benefits. These benefits include greater emotional security, a stronger relationship bond, greater relationship stability, increased stress tolerance, and a greater flow of positive feelings within the relationship.

Couples that trust each other are better able to build and maintain a strong bond together because there is a greater level of emotional security in their relationship. A stronger connection or bond increases relationship stability.

The ability to express positive feelings, particularly love and affection, requires that each partner feel safe and secure with the other partner. Love, affection, and other positive feelings thrive and grow in a relationship that is based on trust. Where there is trust, it is much easier to be vulnerable when expressing nurturance and other forms of caring.

Finally, being in a relationship based on complete trust reduces the overall stress load on the relationship. When a relationship is predictable and reliable there is generally much less concern regarding the stability of the relationship. This allows for a greater tolerance of stress related to the behavior and communication within the relationship.

Benefits Of Trust

- Greater emotional security
- Stronger relationship bond
- Relationship stability
- Better expression of positive feelings
- Improved stress tolerance

Learning To Trust

Basic trust originates in early childhood at a time when one is completely dependent on others to meet one's needs. Trust and emotional security are shaped largely by positive and negative experiences throughout life. If those experiences lead to feeling safe and secure, trust will increase. However, if those experiences lead to frequent or intense frustration, pain, and stress, then feelings of insecurity are much more likely to develop.

Because trust is so important to emotional security, we learn at an early age to identify those qualities that help to determine whom we can trust and whom we cannot. Earlier experiences with trust lead to the formation of a set of beliefs or a trust profile that helps to more quickly determine if someone can be trusted or not. The trust profile generally includes those qualities that allow us to judge others, including physical appearance, behavior, communication, and other qualities that have been associated with trust experiences in the past.

A trust profile can be very accurate in being able to judge others, or it can be extremely inaccurate. Some people have a trust profile that leads them to blindly trust everyone, while others trust no one. Generally, the more that someone's appearance, communication, and behavior align with one's trust profile, the greater the probability that they will be trusted.

The Four Areas of Trust

There are four primary areas of trust in successful relationships. Each of these areas contributes to how much trust each partner has in their partner. The first area of trust is safety. This consists of the belief and feeling that one will not be hurt physically or emotionally in a relationship. A stable level of trust cannot thrive in a relationship where there is physical or emotional insecurity, and particularly if there is any form of abuse, or threat of abuse.

The second area of trust in relationships involves loyalty. This includes physical, emotional, and social loyalty. Successful relationships require loyalty in each of these areas. However, a stable sense of trust rests on the belief that all areas of trust are consistently stable.

A third area of trust involves honesty. Quality relationships require complete honesty and openness to support trust. Without honesty it can be extremely difficult to build and maintain a secure level of trust in a relationship.

Finally, trust requires that each partner in a relationship depend on the other partner to be there for them when needed regardless of the circumstances. Trust requires that each partner believe that the other partner will remain faithful, and not leave or abandon the relationship, particularly during stressful or difficult times.

The Early Foundation of Trust

Trust generally develops slowly over time and largely depends on the experiences each partner shares with the other. In a general sense, trust develops more successfully when each partner's expectations fit the pattern of behavior that each perceives as trustworthy. In essence, trust-related behavior is evaluated in terms of how well the behavior aligns itself with the trust profile that each partner holds.

Being able to fully trust someone requires time to know that someone is honest, loyal, reliable, dependable, and predictable. Generally, the more consistent and predictable these qualities are the faster that trust will tend to develop in the relationship.

One of the best predictors of whether someone can be trusted is how trustworthy they have been in the past. Has there been a history of loyalty, honesty, and dependability in each partner's past relationships? If there have been trust issues in any of these areas in the past, then trust problems are more likely to occur in the future.

The decision to make a lifelong commitment to a partner obviously requires a very high level of trust. Long-term relationships involve many levels of vulnerability and present genuine risks of potential harm to one's mental, emotional, social, and even, financial well-being.

The greatest risks associated with long-term relationships is the potential for relationship failure. The psychological devastation that often follows a relationship breakup can be extremely painful and long-lasting. This can involve countless hours of emotional distress, heartache, and despair that can impact one's well-being for a long period of time. Emotional distress is just one of many risks and consequences associated with a failed relationship. Other significant effects of relationship failure include a negative impact on one's physical and mental health, relationships with family and friends, the ability to function in work, and financial well-being. If children are involved there are often negative long-term consequences for them as well.

Trust is closely connected to many of the other essential needs in a relationship. When the level of trust is secure in a relationship, there will be a positive effect on communication, emotional security, honesty, loyalty, commitment and, most importantly, on the love and happiness shared in the relationship.

On the other hand, problems with trust can also have a negative impact on the other relationship qualities as well. For example, when there is a lack of trust there will often also be a problem with communication, openness, the expression of positive feelings, the ability to solve problems, and in managing the increased stress on the relationship.

Successful vs. Distressed Relationships

As one might predict, there are significant differences between people in quality relationships and those in distressed relationships regarding trust. Couples in successful relationships consistently experience a positive attitude of trust with each other. Successful couples spend very little time on the issue of trust once it is securely established in the relationship.

Couples in distressed relationships, on the other hand, frequently struggle with the issue of trust. They often have problems trusting their partner or, in many cases, have a problem with being trustworthy themselves. As a result, the ability to fully trust each other is disrupted, and is characterized by significant amounts of anxiety, anger, and jealousy.

Another important difference between successful and distressed couples is that successful couples are much better able to talk about

trust issues in a positive and respectful manner. Distressed couples
are much more likely to take a negative approach to trust issues.
Their communication around issues of trust often deteriorates into
anger, accusations, defensiveness, jealousy, and aggressive behavior.

The following qualities reflect the primary differences between
successful and distressed couples.

Successful Relationships

Trustworthy behavior
Openness
Honesty
Reliable
Predictable
Self-disclosure
Positive approach to trust issues
Courage to trust / supportive
Accept and include family and friends
Assumption of loyalty and trust

Distressed Relationships

Untrustworthy behavior
Closed / guarded / secretive
Dishonesty / distortions of fact
Undependable
Unpredictable
Negative statements / accusatory
Unrevealing / withhold information
Negative emotional reactions
Defensive / afraid to trust
Discourage relationships with others
Assumption of guilt

Building Trust

BUILDING trust is an essential part of any relationship. Trust develops primarily through communication and behavior. It involves being consistently honest, loyal, predictable, reliable, and dependable. Trust is based on everything one says and does, all of which has the potential to affect trust.

One of the first and most important steps in building trust is talking about what trust means to each partner. Communication about trust leads to a better understanding of what is most important for each partner to establish a staple level of trust. This provides a better understanding of each partner's expectations related to trust, which plays a major role in establishing a successful foundation for a long-term quality relationship.

Another important factor in building trust is self-disclosure. Sharing important personal information with one's partner is important in the trust building process. Being open with one another regarding any subject helps each partner to understand each other better. This process of opening up with each other helps to strengthen the bond between partners. To encourage self-disclosure, it is important that each partner accept and support the other's expression of how they think and feel without being critical or judgmental.

An essential factor in building trust in a relationship is allowing oneself to be vulnerable. When one partner allows themselves to be vulnerable it encourages the other to be vulnerable as well, which deepens the emotional attachment and level of intimacy. Sue Johnson (2013) offers excellent insights into the nature of trust in romantic relationships and describes how trust is built on small moments of vulnerability and engagement. Allowing oneself to be openly vulnerable, in essence, deepens trust and strengthens a secure attachment.

Gottman and Silver (2015) offer a well-researched approach for building or rebuilding trust in romantic relationships. They focus on the key elements that help to build and recover trust including emotional attunement, turning toward each other instead of away, open communication, managing conflict constructively, consistent reliability and dependability, and commitment to mutual growth.

In essence, building and maintaining trust in a relationship leads to a trust agreement that clearly defines what the expectations of trust mean to each partner. It is important to never assume that there is a trust agreement if it has not been openly talked about. This helps to prevent misunderstandings that can create potential trust problems in the future.

Problems With Trust

Most couples will find a way to resolve their trust issues without too much difficulty. However, many couples will struggle with trust at some point or another. In far too many cases, problems with trust result in a distressed or failed relationship. It is therefore important to resolve all trust problems early in the relationship before they become an entrenched pattern of distrust that can diminish the quality and stability of the relationship.

There are two major sources of trust problems. The first involves trust problems that are currently caused by the behavior of one or both partners. These problems may involve issues of loyalty, dishonesty, not keeping promises, or some other behavior that raises questions about trust.

Common behaviors that are frequently associated with trust problems include lying, secrecy, jealousy, avoiding communication about certain issues, sudden major changes in behavior or appearance, being unreachable, or a significant decrease in caring, intimacy, or affection.

One of the most difficult challenges in any relationship is restoring trust once it has been broken. Infidelity, for instance, can cause such a deep rupture that rebuilding trust may seem impossible. Repairing trust is often a slow process requiring time, effort, and mutual commitment. Cloud (2023) outlines a helpful six-step framework for repairing and rebuilding trust in relationships. His work offers practical guidance for couples struggling with this issue and serves as a valuable resource for those seeking to reestablish genuine and lasting trust in their relationships.

Another major source of trust problems are unresolved problems from past relationships. Past relationship experiences can play a major role in current trust problems. The emotional pain and suffering associated with past disloyalty, hurt, and loss can be emotionally traumatic, difficult to recover from, and often carry over to the next relationship. As a result, a couple may experience significant trust problems in their relationship, even when both partners have been completely trustworthy. It is important to be aware that current trust problems might stem from past experiences related to trust rather than from problems in the current relationship.

Trust problems come at a very high cost to a relationship. The frequent struggle and distress that goes with trust problems often involves an overwhelming amount of work, time, and emotional energy, all of which can lead to a very high stress load on the relationship. The overall stress load associated with chronic trust problems is often far greater than the stress and emotional pain associated with ending the relationship.

In conclusion, trust is one of the most important pillars in the foundation of a happy and successful long-term relationship. Developing and maintaining a solid foundation of trust is essential in protecting the health and future quality of a relationship. Trust develops gradually based on consistent experiences of honesty, loyalty, dependability, and reliability. It requires nurturance and understanding, starting from the beginning of the relationship, and evolving over time, based on experiences related to trust. The effort made to build and maintain a strong foundation of trust will provide one's relationship with many lifelong benefits such as emotional stability, security, reduced stress, and a strong relationship bond that will support a healthy and successful long-term relationship that is full of relationship wealth.

11

LOYALTY
THE TIE THAT BINDS

One of the most important qualities associated with the long-term stability of a healthy relationship is loyalty. The importance of this quality in establishing long-term relationships is significant and is frequently ranked as one of the most important needs by most couples in successful relationships.

Without loyalty, a genuine emotional commitment to a relationship likely does not exist. A relationship without loyalty usually lacks the security and trust needed to withstand the many life challenges that relationships generally endure. For this reason, loyalty, is an essential component of the Green Zone.

Loyalty is often one of the first issues that arise when making the decision to commit to a long-term relationship. For such a major decision to be made, it is essential that there be a sense of security and trust in the person that one is committing to. This essential need will generally determine how well an intimate relationship will develop, grow, and how stable it will remain.

Loyalty, as it applies to intimate relationships, may be defined as an exclusive commitment or agreement to remain faithful to one's partner. It is essentially a promise of fidelity with the expectation that loyalty will be maintained throughout the duration of the relationship. Loyalty is based on the decision and belief that each partner will respect the well-being of each partner's needs in the relationship. In essence, loyalty is essential in building and maintaining successful long-term relationships.

In *The Science of Intimate Relationships*, (Fletcher, et.al. 2013), loyalty is described as a dynamic outcome of commitment, trust, and emotional interdependence between romantic partners. The authors argue that loyalty arises from secure attachment styles, mutual investment, and the belief that a partner is dependable and emotionally responsive. Loyalty, in essence, is supported by both rational and emotional factors.

There are multiple benefits that loyalty provides to a healthy relationship. These benefits include relationship stability, greater emotional security, a stronger emotional bond between partners, greater trust, a more genuine commitment, predictability, and a deeper level of relationship esteem. These core benefits associated with loyalty provide a solid foundation for building and maintaining a long-term relationship.

Loyalty is based on a mutual agreement between partners. This loyalty agreement is based on each partner's needs related to their individual perception of trust and security. For many couples, loyalty is assumed in their relationship. However, loyalty should not be assumed, because it often is a major source of stress when conflict in this area emerges. For this reason, it is important that couples clearly define what each partner needs to commit to a long-term relationship.

Successful relationships are based on several basic agreements between partners. Loyalty is one of the most important agreements necessary for building a successful relationship because it can have a major impact on the quality and stability of a relationship on many levels.

A core component of a successful loyalty agreement is that each partner agrees to provide exclusive faithfulness to the other. Failure to successfully maintain this agreement will place a relationship in jeopardy. Even if the relationship survives the impact of disloyalty, the quality of the relationship will frequently be damaged, leading either to failure or a long recovery period.

The decision to be loyal in a relationship can be a challenging one, especially in the initial phase of the relationship. Making an exclusive commitment to one partner may create an internal conflict for many people. On the one hand there is a desire for security and long-term connection with a partner, while at the same time there may also be a desire for the freedom and the excitement of new relationships. This is particularly true for younger couples who have not been in extended relationships.

The decision to commit exclusively to one person for a lifetime requires a significant amount of time and consideration to be fully confident in making such a serious commitment. Without fully evaluating the consequences of committing one's life to a relationship can make one vulnerable to conflict later. Frequently, couples will agree to being loyal and committed to each other, but they may later have a change of heart.

The decision to exclusively commit to a relationship requires significant thought. Far too often it is made based on emotional impulse instead of thoughts about the potential consequences. For many people this decision is often based much more on emotional factors then practical ones. Strong emotions can lead to wishful or distorted thinking that does not necessarily align itself with reality. It is important to first consider one's own motivation, feelings, and needs. Exploring all possible doubts is an important part of the process.

Types Of Loyalty

Loyalty is often described in terms of physical or sexual fidelity. Physical loyalty involves being sexually faithful exclusively with one's partner. This includes not only sexual behavior, but also includes inappropriate affection, kissing, or touching others in any way that would be considered unacceptable to one's partner. Most people have a relatively clear idea of the boundaries of what is acceptable and appropriate regarding physical intimacy with someone outside of their relationship.

Beyond physical intimacy, there are other types of loyalty that are also important in a relationship. These include emotional, social, financial, and even perhaps spiritual loyalty. It is important that each couple explore each form of loyalty to determine its potential impact on the relationship.

Another type of loyalty involves emotional loyalty. This involves respect for the emotional boundaries between oneself and other emotional relationships. These boundaries are often less clear than physical boundaries. Positive feelings can develop in many different types of relationships. Friendships for example, can consist of a strong bond with deep positive feelings. These positive feelings are often healthy and can help to build a strong social support system. However, conflict can arise when an emotional connection becomes increasingly intimate with someone other than one's partner.

In healthy relationships emotional boundaries are clearly defined. There is an understanding between couples about what is emotionally acceptable and not acceptable in close relationships with others. Both partners understand that close emotional connections can sometimes develop into more personally intimate feelings. Setting clear boundaries helps to prevent these feelings from causing issues that can undermine loyalty. This helps to create a greater degree of freedom that allows one to form deep emotional connections to others without it being a threat to the stability of the relationship.

Another area of loyalty that can be a source of conflict is social loyalty. This involves making the social needs of one's partner a priority over the needs in other social relationships. This usually involves deciding how much time to spend with one's partner, as opposed to time with family, friends, and others. Successful couples generally seek to establish a balance in which the needs of their relationship come first, followed by the needs of other social relationships.

Social loyalty can also involve how one partner treats the other in social situations. This generally consists of how one partner talks to the other partner in the presence of others. It may also include how one partner talks to others about their partner. For example, as a couple, do they talk to or about each other in positive ways, or are they critical or negative to each other in social situations?

Another form of loyalty consists of financial loyalty. This type of loyalty involves being open and honest about the management of financial resources. This may include issues related to undisclosed debts, credit card charges, hidden expenses, secret accounts, and acquiring assets without the other partners knowledge. It is important that couples fully disclose financial issues with each other so that problems in this area can be avoided.

A less frequent type of loyalty is spiritual or religious loyalty. In this case, one partner may have an expectation that certain religious or spiritual beliefs will be followed by the other partner. For example, one partner may have the expectation that the other partner will convert to their religious beliefs. When these expectations are not supported or practiced, it may be viewed as a form of spiritual disloyalty.

Types of Loyalty

- Physical / Sexual
- Emotional
- Social
- Financial
- Spiritual

Loyalty In Successful and Distressed Relationships

There are significant differences regarding loyalty between

couples in quality relationships compared to those in distressed relationships. In quality relationships, loyalty is clearly defined so that each partner's needs are expressed in a way that enables clear boundaries to be established in the relationship. These relationship boundaries are consistently respected and maintained, which provides greater stability and trust in the relationship. Successful couples also place a much greater emphasis on prevention. They can openly discuss potential conflicts or problem areas that have the potential to occur in the future. They are free to express their anxiety and insecurity related to any issue that may potentially become a problem in their relationship.

Successful couples demonstrate a greater awareness and empathy regarding how hurtful disloyalty would be to their partner and how damaging it would be to their relationship. They understand the emotional impact and consequences of disloyalty. For these reasons there is a mutual desire to honor the commitment and protect their relationship. Because of this there is an ever-present awareness of the need to honor and protect their commitment together and the boundaries of their relationship.

Because of successful couples' efforts to establish a clear agreement regarding loyalty, the issue generally remains in the background and requires little attention or discussion on an ongoing basis. As a result, loyalty is rarely a source of concern or distress in the relationship because the boundaries are clear, and issues are addressed early before becoming a problem that can harm the relationship.

Couples in distressed relationships, on the other hand, often struggle regarding loyalty issues. There is often significant anxiety and distress surrounding this issue. Because the relationship is in distress there is often an underlying fear that the potential for disloyalty is more likely to occur, particularly if there have been loyalty problems in the past. In this case every outside relationship may be seen as a potential threat.

In distressed relationships the connections and emotional boundaries are often unclear and ambiguous, which can often lead to strong feelings of insecurity. As a result, the lack of clear relationship boundaries can further increase feelings of insecurity, jealousy, resentment, and anger that can lead to negative behavior and potential disloyalty. Over time, this emotional pattern can erode the quality of the relationship, eventually leading to instability and a greater probability of relationship failure.

Emotional insecurity and the threat of disloyalty can be a significant problem for many couples even when there has not been any violation of trust or loyalty. Frequently the cause of this is that one or both partners have experienced disloyalty in a past relationship. Due to the traumatic nature of that experience, there is often significant concern that they may be betrayed again. This is especially true for couples who are in unhappy or unstable relationships. As the relationship becomes more unstable each partner's anxiety potentially increases regarding disloyalty.

When disloyalty occurs, many relationships do not survive the emotional trauma that it causes. Others will continue but will require a significant amount of work to restore relationship stability to a functional level again. For most of these relationships there will not be the same level of trust that existed prior to the event that broke the trust. Couples trying to work through problems with disloyalty will need good communication to resolve this issue. Very often communication was a problem to begin with and may have played a role in the increased risk of disloyalty. In this case, it is often beneficial to get counseling to help improve the communication and restore the relationship. In any event, the road back to stability will require a great deal of care and reassurance over a significant period of time.

Loyalty is clearly one of the major core needs in successful relationships. There are significant feelings of security associated with loyalty. As is the case with most of the other essential needs in a successful relationship, loyalty problems will also have a significant impact on every other relationship need, but particularly the needs for trust, honesty, commitment, love, and nurturance.

Loyalty is one of the key pillars of successful relationships. The importance of having a solid and clear loyalty agreement is essential for maintaining stability in a relationship. The importance of establishing clear boundaries around this issue cannot be understated. Building and maintaining loyalty is a deeply personal and core need for couples. Successful couples are not only able to create an effective loyalty agreement, but they also see loyalty as essential to building a long-term healthy and secure relationship.

12

RESPECT

THE SILENT LANGUAGE OF LOVE

Respect is an essential need in all quality relationships. It is the golden thread that runs through the foundation of all successful relationships. But what exactly does respect mean? And why is respect so important to quality relationships?

In a general sense, respect is the act of showing high regard for the needs, rights, and dignity of others. Respect within an intimate relationship is based on the idea that each partner has the right to be treated with the highest level of positive regard or care. Successful relationships are based on the belief or principal that each partner should be treated with the highest level of respect so that the well-being and integrity of the relationship is preserved.

Generally, respect involves any behavior or communication that treats one's partner in a positive and fair manner. This includes any positive action or communication that show recognition, attention, and consideration for the well-being of one's partner. It acknowledges and honors their needs, ideas, feelings, and interests. In essence, respect includes everything that you say and do that builds or maintains the quality and stability of the relationship.

Respect is also closely related to acceptance, which involves not only the acceptance of one's partner for who they are as a person, but also the many factors and qualities that are a part of them. In essence, acceptance allows each partner to be themselves without judgement and criticism.

The importance of respect in romantic relationships is essential to building and maintaining a health long-term relationship. One study found that respect can be a stronger predictor of relationship satisfaction than love or liking alone (Young and Zeigler-Hill, 2024). The lack of respect, as expected, is generally associated with lower relationship satisfaction and is often an important reason for relationship failure.

One of the major reasons that respect is so important to a quality relationship is because it reflects how much each partner values the other and highlights the importance of the relationship to them. Respect in a relationship, or the lack of respect toward one's partner, serves as an important measure of the overall health of a relationship. For these reasons, respect is an essential component of the Green Zone.

Respect conveys a sense of equality and fairness in one's relationship, which creates a relationship environment where positive feelings can develop, flourish, and grow. Respect and acceptance both contribute to the long-term quality and stability of a successful relationship.

Types Of Respect

Respect plays an important role in healthy relationships in multiple ways. Generally, there are three types of respect that are important to a successful relationship. These include respect for oneself, respect for one's partner, and respect for the needs of the relationship. Each type of respect is interrelated, and together they play an important role in maintaining a healthy relationship.

The first type of respect is self-respect. To effectively respect one's partner, it is essential to first have self-respect. Respect for oneself, in essence, involves taking care of personal needs so that there is less stress and dependency on one's partner. A partner that takes excellent care of themselves is more likely to take care of their partner.

Self-respect is based in how one views themselves, which in turn determines the level of care they provide to themselves. It involves recognizing that your life has value and that you deserve to be treated with care and respect. This self-awareness often makes one more attractive to one's partner.

People who have a high-level of self-respect generally have a clear understanding of their personal, physical, emotional, and social needs. As a result, they are more likely to meet their own needs in a healthy manner. They are also more likely to do those things that maintain health such as eating healthy, exercising, or getting enough rest.

Self-respect also involves taking care of yourself by avoiding unhealthy behavior, thinking, or relationships. Negative thinking for example can often lead to negative or unhealthy behavior, such as excessive drinking, which can then create new problems and put additional stress on a relationship.

From another perspective, would you want your partner to have little respect for themselves? Do you really want to be with someone who doesn't take care of themselves, who doesn't value their own self-worth? A partner who respects themselves tends to bring a stronger, more balanced attitude to the relationship. In essence, a partner who cares for themselves is more likely to care more deeply for their partner.

Another form of respect is social respect, which is a key factor of social intelligence and emotional maturity. The level of respect that one shows to a partner is one of the most significant factors in determining the quality and stability of a relationship.

Respect for one's partner requires the acceptance of them as a complete person. This means accepting both their positive and negative qualities, their flaws, and the many differences that they have that are different from one's own.

Respect involves encouraging one's partner to exercise the right to be themselves. This encourages them to express their own unique ideas on any subject. It also places a high value on their needs, feelings and ideas. Acknowledging their viewpoint creates a sense of equality and freedom that enriches the relationship.

Being respectful does not necessarily mean that you agree with a particular idea or viewpoint. However, it does mean that you are willing to accept a different point of view. Most couples disagree on many issues. But it is important to disagree in a respectful way. Respecting the differences between partners allows each partner the freedom to express their feelings and ideas without fear of negative judgment.

Respect for one's partner also means being considerate of their time, privacy, and independence. Each partner has the right to use their time in ways that meet their independent needs while also addressing the needs of the relationship. Recognizing the need for time to pursue personal interests is essential for personal growth. Additionally, it is important for each partner to have adequate alone time to recharge personally.

Respect may also mean accepting one's partner's need to maintain relationships with their family and friends. A strong social network is healthy for a relationship in that it provides emotional support and opportunities for personal growth. By encouraging each other to maintain family and other social relationships, partners create a balance that enriches their lives together.

Respect also includes encouraging and supporting a partner's dreams and interests. Partners may not always share the same dreams, but it is important that they support and encourage each other's passions and dreams. This creates an environment of trust and support, allowing both partners to grow individually and together.

Another form of respect is supporting the way that one's partner communicates or expresses themselves. Respect for the way in which a partner communicates is in essence a form of caring and nurturance. Partners who encourage each other to fully express themselves without criticism or judgment are generally going to be much more successful in maintaining a successful relationship.

Another important type of respect involves the respect for the needs of the relationship. By understanding relationship needs and placing a high value on them, couples are much more likely to establish and maintain a stable and healthy relationship. In this case, emphasis is not so much on each other but on the needs of the relationship. Instead, the focus is on improving the quality of communication, improving nurturance, resolving problems, and managing stress successfully.

There are times when respect for the relationship must override the needs of each partner for the sake of stability. Placing the needs of the relationship ahead of one's own needs can be a challenging but necessary sacrifice. This often involves the acceptance of ideas, desires, and views that are significantly different from one's own.

Respect almost always involves acceptance or compromise. However, there are times where there can be no compromise but require total sacrifice to make a particular situation work. The amount of sacrifice made by each partner to meet the needs of the relationship is itself a very important form of caring that will have a direct impact on the quality and stability of the relationship.

Successful vs. Distressed Relationships

Respect is one of the more critical qualities that separates successful relationships from distressed relationships. People in healthy long-term relationships are consistently more respectful of the needs, feelings, ideas, and well-being of their partners. What stands out most is that they can consistently maintain a high level of respect for each other even during periods of significant conflict and stress. Despite the emotional stress level, they are still able to maintain a high level of respect for their partners.

Respect is generally expressed through communication and behavior. This includes anything that one says or does to show that one's partner is important and highly regarded. For example, when one partner tells the other that they appreciate them, or that they are happy to have them in their life, they are in essence expressing respect and caring for them. Even when one partner criticizes the other, if done in a positive and supportive way, one can still convey respect.

One of the most significant ways to express respect is through listening. Fully listening to one's partner shows them that one really values what they have to say. Listening without interruption is one of the highest forms of respect in that it allows one's partner to fully express themselves, which allows them to feel respected. Listening acknowledges the needs, feelings, and ideas of one's partner in a nonjudgmental way. This is an essential part of respect in a healthy relationship.

Respect can also be expressed between partners through their behavior. This can take many forms. Some examples include when one partner helps the other with chores, does extra things for them, or takes care of them when they are not feeling well.

Couples in distressed relationships generally do not express a level of respect necessary to sustain a healthy relationship. They often show little or no respect for each other. More typically, they can convey marginal levels of respect during periods of low stress but as stress increases disrespect and contempt become the norm. Consequently, they tend to be more critical, sarcastic, or hurtful to each other, which leads to a decrease in the quality and stability of relationships.

Many of the major problems in relationships can often be traced back to a lack of respect. Problems by their nature present high levels of emotional stress. However, it is often the attitude of disrespect that leads to the greatest instability in relationships. A disrespectful approach to one's problems can turn even the simplest problem into a major issue. Even in those cases where the problem gets worked out, negative feelings often remain long after the problem was addressed.

Establishing an attitude of respect provides numerous benefits to the health of a relationship. On an individual level, partners with self-respect tend to practice better self-care and encourage each other to do the same, which promotes personal growth and enhances relationship stability.

Couples who show respect for one another benefit by feeling more accepted, valued, and appreciated. When partners show mutual respect, they create an opportunity for a deeper engagement with each other. Respect reinforces love and commitment in the relationship. Couples who consistently show respect for each other enjoy greater trust, harmony, and emotional intimacy.

Another key benefit of mutual respect is that it provides greater stability and security in a relationship. Respect creates an environment where both partners feel comfortable expressing their needs, which in turn makes it easier to fulfill and satisfy those needs. As a result, there is the benefit of contributing to a more stable and peaceful relationship environment.

Finally, respect has a protective benefit by reducing the likelihood of conflict, tension, and stress. In essence, mutual respect reduces communication and behavior that have the potential to reduce relationship stability and damage the relationship bond.

Respect provides many benefits that have a direct impact on building and maintaining relationship wealth. Mutual respect offers a multitude of benefits that contribute to the long-term health of a relationship. On the other hand, disrespect is a major source of stress on an intimate relationship that can dramatically increase the risk of relationship failure.

Developing respect for oneself, for one's partner, or respect for the needs of a relationship can be learned and improved by anyone with a desire to do so. The first step is to identify those areas where there is a need to improve the level of respect. Asking one's partner if they feel respected and where they desire greater respect is a good starting point.

Respect is clearly one of the major pillars of a healthy life-long relationship. Every partner deserves to be treated with respect as it represents the highest level of care and love that one partner can share with another. In essence, respect is a gift that we can freely share with our partner. Ultimately, it is one of the more important pathways to achieving a satisfying and fulfilling long-term relationship.

13

HONESTY

THE PURIST FORM OF INTIMACY

F ew would argue that honesty is not a critically important need in all relationships. The ability to effectively meet relationship needs and to maintain the stability of a relationship requires openness and honesty. Honesty is the bedrock that supports the entire relationship. It is an essential component of the Green Zone. Without honesty there will be no trust or security.

According to a recent survey of relationship values, couples ranked honesty as the second most important value in a relationship, preceded only by trust (YouGov, 2025). Without honesty the entire foundation of a relationship becomes unstable and fragile.

Most people would agree that honesty is essential in a relationship. But does that mean that couples in successful relationships are always completely honest and completely accurate in everything they say and do in their relationships? Is it even possible to be totally honest in every sense of the word? Based on the communication of couples in both successful and distressed relationships, it becomes clear that it is not possible to achieve absolute honesty. There are just too many factors that limit the accuracy of communication to guarantee that one's communication will be honest on every level.

However, there are clear boundaries as to what constitutes honest and clear communication.

It is important to start with an accurate definition or description of what honesty is as it relates to intimate relationships. In general, honesty in this context can be defined as the quality that allows information to be communicated in an accurate and truthful manner from one partner to the other. Honesty includes the open and direct expression of all relevant facts and information about any given subject. It is based on a genuine belief that the facts are true to the best of one's knowledge.

The Distinction Between Truth and Honesty

In defining honesty, it is important to draw a distinction between honesty and truth. Truth can be considered an absolute and is based totally on the facts of reality. There is generally only one truth, although there can be many interpretations of the truth. Honesty, on the other hand, is an interpretation of truth based on an understanding of the facts as each partner perceives them. As a result, it is possible to have different versions of the truth based on the information that each person has available to them.

There are many situations where it is not possible to know the complete truth because not every fact is available or known. Even when all the facts are known it is easy to misinterpret them, which leads to a distortion of the truth. As a result, one may truly believe that they are being honest but, because of their misinterpretation of the facts, they are not accurately reflecting the truth. The question then is not if partners distort the truth, but how much distortion there is and how much it contributes to relationship misunderstandings.

One of the most important distinctions that can be made is whether the distortion of truth is intentional or unintentional. By far, the most frequent distortion that occurs in communication is unintentional. This distortion effect often occurs without either partner being aware that they are misunderstanding the other.

One of the main reasons for distortion of the truth is the limited nature of relationship communication itself. Words are often unclear, vague, or open to many possible interpretations. They frequently fail to convey the true meaning of what is intended. For example, think of the many variations that there are on the word "love." What one partner means when they use the word love can be quite different from what their partner means.

Another major cause of distortion in communication between partners is emotion. Anger, fear, and hurt can often lead to significant distortion in the way that partners think and communicate with each other. These emotions play a powerful role in how accurate communication is, and are often a major reason for chronic misunderstandings in relationships.

Despite the amount of distortion that can exist in communication, most couples are still able to communicate with each other successfully most of the time. The most important factor for this success is that they each can trust and rely on the other to be intentionally honest. This basic trust and faith of each partner in the honesty of the other helps to compensate for the inadequacy of words and emotional misunderstandings that are an inevitable part of communication in intimate relationships.

The Importance of Honesty

The fact that honesty is such an important factor in quality relationships is no surprise. It provides many important benefits to building and maintaining a successful relationship. Almost certainly, the most important benefit is better communication. For communication to be clear, accurate, and believable, it is necessary for there to be honesty and openness. Honesty not only helps to improve the quality of the communication, but it also can reduce the frequency of misunderstandings. As a result, there is much less stress on the relationship, which enhances its overall stability.

If the primary goal of communication is to understand and meet relationship needs, then honest communication is a critical condition necessary to achieve that goal. Effective communication, therefore, requires honest and accurate information so that there can be a clear understanding of the meaning of the communication between partners.

Another important reason that honesty is so important for a successful long-term relationship is that it is directly related to trust and feelings of security. A strong and stable foundation of trust in a relationship requires honest and open communication between partners. If someone's honesty is in question, it becomes almost impossible to maintain a sense of trust and security in the relationship.

Honesty is also necessary for a successful relationship because it increases emotional closeness. The open and honest expression of what one thinks and feels, especially regarding intimate details, is necessary to establish and maintain feelings of closeness in a relationship. Emotional closeness is deeper when a partner feels that they can be fully open about themselves and still be accepted and loved.

A University of Rochester study involving over 200 couples found that honesty when expressed by one partner and accurately perceived by the other significantly improved both individual and relationship well-being. (Le, B.M., et.al. 2025). In essence, when partners are honest with each other, even with uncomfortable subjects, they are more motivated to change and meet each other's needs.

Successfully solving relationship problems and managing emotional stress also rely on honest communication. When one partner says one thing and then does something else it creates unnecessary stress on the relationship. It makes solving problems that much more difficult.

Although the unintentional distortion of the truth occurs in all relationships to some extent, it is the intentional distortion of the truth that causes the most damage. Many relationship conflicts are a direct result of one partner intentionally distorting the truth or not fully disclosing information to the other partner. This pattern of dishonesty can rapidly become a cancer to the health of a relationship.

In general, most couples tend to be relatively honest with each other. However, there are many subjects, especially emotionally sensitive subjects, that cause a great deal of stress on one or both partners. It is usually regarding these more emotionally sensitive subjects that distortion occurs and honesty is challenged.

Successful vs. Distressed Relationships

As expected, there are significant differences between couples in successful relationships and those in distressed relationships regarding honesty and openness. All couples will at one time, or another distort, exaggerate, minimize, or enhance facts and information. However, the frequency and degree of distortion is generally much greater among people in distressed relationships.

Couples in distressed relationships often will distort what they say, both unintentionally and intentionally. Consequently, they experience a far greater amount of stress on their relationships. Once a pattern of intentional distortion develops within a relationship it often spreads across many other areas of the relationship. If a partner tends to distort the truth in one subject area, they are much more likely to distort the truth in other areas as well.

Partners in distressed relationships are also much more likely to omit facts or parts of a story that are not favorable to them. Although intentionally distorting the truth or intentionally omitting facts is essentially lying, many partners in distressed relationships may not consider it to be so.

A pattern of intentionally distorting the truth with one's partner is ultimately going to lead to a failed relationship. For this reason, it is essential that couples strive to be open and honest with each other in order to protect their relationship from this unhealthy pattern of communication.

Most couples in successful relationships are very much aware of how destructive dishonest communication can be to their relationship and actively work to avoid distorted and dishonest communication that would be harmful to their relationship. It is important to strive for open, honest, and direct communication to meet the needs of each partner and to help prevent a pattern of dishonest communication from developing within the relationship.

Couples in successful relationships consistently strive to be honest and open in their relationships. They make every effort to present the truth based on the facts as they know them. As a result, their communication flows automatically and in a more direct, authentic, and believable manner. Although truth can unintentionally be distorted in all relationships, the intentional distortion of the truth is a much greater problem in distressed relationships. As a result, couples in distressed relationships frequently "second guess" what their partner says and find it difficult to maintain a healthy level of trust.

Successful Relationships

Honesty
Minimal distortion
Lower frequency of distortion
Open and direct
Self-disclosure
Seeks truth
Encourage conflict resolution
Much better understanding of partner

Distressed Relationships

Dishonesty
Intentional distortion / Lying
Greater frequency of distortion
Indirect meaning
Closed / guarded
Avoids truth
Conflict avoidance
Limited understanding of partner

Common Reasons for Dishonesty

Individuals in distressed relationships are more likely to intentionally distort facts, make false statements, and withhold information. There are generally two major reasons that partners intentionally distort facts or withhold information from each other. The first reason is there is some benefit that they want but have not been able to gain through honest or direct communication. The second major reason for a lack of honesty is fear and anxiety, driven by the desire to avoid conflict or some negative consequence or outcome.

The avoidance of conflict is one of the most common patterns of couples in distressed relationships. Many believe that avoiding conflict is the best way to maintain a stable relationship. However, in the long run, the avoidance of conflict can be extremely costly to a relationship because the underlying causes of conflict are not resolved, and they continue to cause chronic distress. As a result, this problem ultimately leads to a much greater stress load on the relationship.

How Honesty Can Improve a Relationship

- Improves communication
- Better able to resolve problems
- More durable solutions
- Decreased stress
- Greater relationship esteem
- Deeper level of trust
- Emotional closeness
- Relationship stability

Talking about problems in an intimate relationship can be difficult and stressful. Everyone has their own perspective, and they can frequently be different from each other. By their nature, relationship problems can be difficult to talk about. Being able to talk openly about sex, money, in-laws, sharing chores, and other problems can be a significant challenge for many couples.

One of the key differences between people in successful relationships and those in distressed relationships is the ability to openly talk about all subjects, including those that generate significant conflict or distress. Instead of avoiding stressful subjects, couples in successful relationships are much more willing to take them on directly.

Couples in successful relationships, like those in distressed relationships, can also be emotionally reactive. However, a major difference is that they are better able to express directly and honestly what they think and feel with each other, while at the same time maintaining respect for each other.

Open and honest communication about relationship problems and needs provides many positive benefits to a healthy relationship. It increases the likelihood of resolving problems, reduces stress, strengthens respect, and cultivates a deeper engagement between partners.

Openness In Successful Relationships

Openness is an important dimension of honesty. Openness refers to the degree to which partners can freely share their personal feelings, beliefs, and needs with each other. The ability to be completely open with one's partner is an essential quality found in all quality long-term relationships. Openness and self-disclosure allow couples to know each other at a deeper and more intimate level.

The lack of openness is one of the most common problems found in distressed relationships. The inability to express one's feelings, needs, and desires is one of the leading causes of misunderstandings and problems in relationships. It is extremely difficult to meet a partner's needs if the partner is not open about them.

As with dishonesty, a lack of openness come at a high cost to a relationship. It creates more work, more stress, more conflict, and many more hours of emotional distress. A lack of openness can result in a relationship that is in a chronic state of distress, instability, and insecurity.

Generally, most couples strive to be open and honest with each other. And when there is dishonesty, it usually involves a specific area. For example, one partner may not completely disclose financial information, or another may not share information about alcohol or gambling. Another example would be a partner's unspoken desire for more affection because they do not want to appear needy or selfish. These examples demonstrate that dishonesty or a lack of openness can be specific or general, subtle or blatant, and intentional or unintentional.

Honesty issues often stem from anxiety or fear, making it hard to address relationship problems. The solution to this problem is to foster an environment where both partners feel free to express themselves. Without this, it can be difficult for partners to better understand each other's needs.

It is important that couples in successful relationships continue to strive to maintain openness and honesty in all aspects of their relationship. However, this does not mean that all honesty is acceptable, particularly when it may cause harm to one's partner. For example, frequently reminding one's partner of some negative aspect of themselves may be honest but can also be hurtful. This pattern of "toxic honesty" is more often found in distressed relationships than in successful ones. If some emotionally negative truth needs to be shared, then it is best to present it in a way that minimizes harm while still preserving the truth.

Finally, couples in successful relationships understand a simple and basic fact of relationships - that open and honest communication about what one truly thinks, feels, and needs ultimately leads to a much more stable and meaningful long-term relationship.

Improving Honesty and Openness in Communication

HONESTY AND OPENNESS are clearly essential to building and maintaining a quality relationship. However, many couples that are aware that honesty or a lack of openness is a problem but may not know how to change or improve this pattern of communication.

The first step is prioritizing openness and honesty in the relationship. This requires an agreement for both partners to unconditionally support and encourage each other's expression of thoughts, feelings, and needs.

To improve openness and honesty, it is important that each partner feels secure in sharing their deepest feelings, desires, and needs. Criticism and other negative responses must be avoided. Otherwise, the process can break down and lead to withholding information and a dishonest pattern of communication.

Do to the fact that so many issues related to honesty are specific, it is important to first identify the areas where it has been difficult to be completely open with one's partner. It is then important to determine what it is about the particular area or subject that makes it difficult to be honest or open about. Once the fears or anxieties regarding the subject are identified, it is important to think about how best to express this anxiety more openly. It is helpful to remember that on the other side of honesty and openness is a greater intimacy and engagement that can ultimately strengthen the relationship.

Developing open and honest communication is a continuous process that requires practice. Over time, this effort can ultimately replace avoidance patterns that can lead to distrust. Each challenging problem should be seen as an opportunity to strengthen communication in the relationship.

To encourage openness and honesty in a relationship, both partners must genuinely encourage and accept each other's ideas, feelings, and needs without judgement or criticism. Although it can be difficult to accept differing viewpoints, doing so is essential for building intimacy and stability.

In summary, honesty is essential in building a strong and lasting relationship. It provides greater trust, security, emotional closeness, better communication and less conflict, and ultimately improve relationship stability. Though it may be challenging at times, developing a consistent pattern of honesty is crucial for maintaining a healthy and satisfying long-term relationship. Doing so is the essence of building relationship wealth.

14

FAIRNESS

THE GIFT OF GENEROSITY

One of the most important qualities in a stable and healthy long-term relationship is fairness. It is extremely difficult to maintain a healthy relationship when one or both partners feel that the relationship is not fair. A lack of fairness is often a common cause of distress in relationships and frequently at the root of many recurrent conflicts.

Fairness is an essential pillar in the foundation of strong, enduring relationships. It is a critical part of building relationship wealth. Fairness influences nearly every interaction between partners. It contributes directly to the stability and health of a relationship by providing a balance between the interests and needs of each partner in the relationship. For this reason, fairness is an essential component of the Green Zone.

For our purposes, fairness may be defined as the expectation that what one contributes to a relationship will be reciprocated in a way that is balanced and equitable, either directly or indirectly. If both partners agree that a situation is fair, it can be said that fairness has been achieved.

Fairness is based on the idea that there is a reasonably equal and balanced distribution of benefits, resources, and responsibilities within the relationship. How well each partner supports the other's needs in a fair way has a direct impact on whether the relationship is perceived as fair by each partner.

Most of our expectations about close relationships are grounded in the concept of fairness. Fairness plays a major role in problem solving, conflict management, dividing chores and responsibilities, spending time and money, and even expressing love.

There are several essential benefits that fairness provides. These benefits include greater relationship stability, emotional closeness, satisfaction of needs, and an increased motivation to compromise and share responsibilities. Fairness also helps to protect a relationship by preventing unhealthy levels of stress to accrue in the relationship.

Most successful relationships are not fair in every aspect, nor are they based on each partner contributing equally to all areas. Fairness is determined in various ways. What may seem unfair to an outsider might be balanced and compensated for in other ways within the relationship. For example, one partner may always do the dishes and manages finances or tasks that the first partner prefers not to do.

Fairness is a broad concept that influences many aspects of a relationship. More importantly, its impact on a relationship is cumulative over time. Ultimately, what matters most is that both partners perceive the pattern of giving and receiving as fair over the course of their relationship and that it aligns with the expectations of both partners as to what is fair.

A key factor in perceiving fairness in a relationship is each partner's attitude toward it. When partners express a genuine desire to be fair, it can help to counterbalance many situations that might otherwise be deemed as unfair. This attitude or desire to be as fair as possible is itself, a form of caring within the relationship.

The belief that a relationship is fair rests on the principal of reciprocity. Reciprocity is the process of giving and receiving in a way that is acceptable to both partners. It is based on the expectation that when something is given, then there will be an equivalent effort by the other partner to give back something of equal or comparable value. This may include the exchange of money, gifts, responsibilities and, most importantly, love and affection.

In general, there is a common expectation that if there is an increase or decrease in giving or caring by one partner, it will lead to a reciprocal increase or decrease in giving or caring in the other partner. In essence, how much one partner gives will generally tend to lead the other partner to respond in a similar manner. Reciprocity helps to maintain a fair balance of giving and receiving within the relationship.

Relationship problems often arise when significant imbalances in fairness continue for a prolonged period, particularly when one partner receives much more than they give in return. This imbalance in the fair exchange of resources can often lead to distress and a decline in caring from the other partner, eventually creating a strain on the relationship.

Fairness in a relationship is based on the equitable sharing of resources, including time, energy, and finances. The perception of fairness often depends on each partner's willingness to contribute in proportion to the resources that they have received. It is based more on an individual's ability to contribute, rather than simply dividing resources equally.

For fairness to be genuinely achieved in a relationship, both partners must come to an agreement on a broad range of issues. This includes dividing chores, managing bills, caring for children, resolving conflicts, and handling stress. Each of these areas requires mutual understanding and cooperation to ensure that the agreements reached are perceived as fair and reasonable by both partners.

Couples often experience significant differences in the way in which they see fairness regarding specific issues. What one partner thinks is fair may differ greatly from the other's viewpoint. These disagreements often result in increased conflict and stress within the relationship.

To address differences in partners' views of fairness requires first understanding each partner's perspective. This lays the foundation for compromise and the adjustments necessary to achieve a balanced view of fairness. The ability to negotiate and compromise on issues of fairness is essential for maintaining relationship stability.

When looking at successful couples one key factor stands out - generosity. This is evident not only by their conception of fairness but, more importantly, their desire to give more than what would normally be perceived as just, or adequate. This is further strengthened by the consistent effort to put their partner's needs before their own. It is this attitude of generosity that provides a greater level of quality and stability to healthy relationships.

Successful relationships thrive when both partners focus more on giving than on receiving. Instead of focusing on measuring the value of what they receive, they focus on the deeper satisfaction that they get from contributing to their partner's happiness. Over time, this mutual generosity builds a stronger bond, which nurtures a supportive and lasting engagement.

A key difference between distressed and successful couples is that distressed couples focus much more time struggling with the issue of fairness. They are preoccupied more with what they receive rather than what they give. They are also more sensitive and emotionally reactive when they do not get what they perceive as fair share. The general attitude of each partner in a distressed relationship is one that reflects an unwillingness to give unless there is some benefit to be gained.

Improving Fairness

Improving fairness in a relationship begins with open and honest communication. Both partners need to be open with each other about any issue that they believe to be unfair. Given the sensitivity of these issues, it's important for each partner to maintain a supportive attitude and to respect the other partner's viewpoints. The most effective way for a partner to address these concerns is to clearly explain their viewpoint while also listening with an open mind to their partner's perspective. This approach creates a pathway toward understanding, which can lead to compromise and agreement.

Sometimes issues of fairness are based on a misunderstanding and can be resolved quickly with a simple agreement. At other times, changes in fairness happen more gradually and require patience. The goal is to make the situation fairer, even if it is not perfect.

The process of negotiating a fair agreement is very often an emotionally challenging process that requires the mutual support and respect of each partner. The focus should be on what each partner can give, rather than on what they may be losing or sacrificing. This shift in thinking, where the focus is on giving, is a key difference that separates couples in successful relationships from those in distress. While learning to give generously in the spirit of fairness can be difficult, the benefits of a balanced and fair relationship far outweigh the sacrifice and compromises involved.

Establishing a fair and successful agreement focuses on shared responsibility. Rodsky (2019) offers a practical framework for dividing and managing physical, emotional, and mental labor fairly. This approach empowers couples to move from resentment or imbalance toward a more successful collaborative partnership.

Acceptance

The goal of all healthy relationships is to strive toward fairness in meeting each partner's needs. However, achieving complete fairness in every aspect of a relationship is not always possible. For this reason, the ability to accept that certain aspects of a relationship may not change is often an essential part of intimate relationships. Fairness and acceptance are closely related. Since each partner has unique needs and, at times, incompatible differences, it's important for couples to find ways to adapt and accept these differences. Many of these differences may even be difficult or undesirable, but learning to adapt and accept them is essential for achieving a long-term quality relationship.

It's not uncommon for a partner to have one or more undesirable qualities that the other partner will need to accept. Many of these differences may be minor and can be adapted to through compromise. However, some differences can be much more difficult and may seem impossible to accept. The ability to adapt to or accept these differences is one of the most difficult challenges for couples to work through together.

Common areas of conflict in relationships often include issues related to family and social relationships, decisions about child rearing, financial management, and career concerns. Other challenges may involve accepting undesirable physical traits. Negative habits or behaviors, like poor self-care, gambling, or excessive drinking, can cause tension. In other cases, there may be personality traits such as temper reactions or selfishness that can be a significant source of stress, leading to conflict in the relationship.

It is neither possible nor necessarily desirable to be equal or perfectly compatible with one's partner in every aspect. One partner may earn more money, have more energy, be better educated, or be better at managing certain problems. These differences can present challenges in the process of adapting to or accepting one's partner.

The ability to accept challenging or negative qualities in one's partner is determined by several factors. These include how undesirable the specific quality is, how realistic is it for the quality to change, the amount of distress the quality causes and, finally, the attitude and willingness to compromise or make changes.

When one partner excessively focuses on the other's undesirable qualities it suggests a lack acceptance. This is often interpreted by the other partner as a sign of not being cared for. In response, they may also begin to focus on the negative aspects of the other partner or, even, the relationship itself, which can lead to a cycle of dissatisfaction and, ultimately, the failure of the relationship.

The ability to accept differences in one's partner or the relationship often requires a certain degree of tolerance. This may involve tolerating annoying qualities such as snoring, eating habits, or how chores are done. It could also involve tolerating differences in politics, religion, or other opinions. Tolerance can also involve dealing with a partner's difficult family members or friends that are a challenge to get along with. In other cases, it might mean being willing to participate in activities that hold little or no interest. In all these situations, some degree of tolerance or acceptance is necessary to maintain stability, fairness, and balance in the relationship.

Sometimes acceptance involves dealing with problems from the past. These may include issues regarding previous relationships, children from a previous marriage, or past behavior that is disturbing or hard to accept. Although these issues may be difficult to accept, they must be adapted to, as nothing can be done in the present moment to change the past.

Sometimes past problems can carry over and continue to affect a problem in the present. For example, insecurities about loyalty in the current relationship may stem from past experiences of disloyalty. Other issues, such as financial concerns, conflicts with in-laws, difficulties managing disagreements, child rearing practices, or even decisions about household responsibilities, can carry over to a new relationship. Each of these areas may require attention and acceptance for the relationship to progress in a positive direction and maintaining its fairness.

Even though acceptance is crucial in all healthy relationships, it has its limits. Some differences are unacceptable and can harm the well-being of the relationship. Issues such as disloyalty, broken trust, physical abuse, or dishonesty make it extremely difficult, if not impossible, to build or sustain a healthy, long-term relationship. In such cases, tolerance and acceptance can harm the relationship. Unfortunately, many people tolerate and endure this behavior, hoping it will change over time. However, acceptance of these issues with the expectation of future improvement rarely leads to a successful outcome.

Change and acceptance is an ongoing process throughout the lifespan of a relationship. Changes in career, relocating, raising children, and facing a range of other issues will require adaptation and acceptance. These challenges will require compromise and acceptance. At times, this may mean adjusting to an entirely new way of life. Sometimes it will mean letting go of things that are familiar and feel safe. However, these challenges also present opportunities for growth and intimacy, ultimately leading to greater emotional satisfaction and relationship stability.

Genuine acceptance and fairness involve the ability and desire to see one's partner as they truly are, rather than as some ideal version of a partner. Acceptance of a partner's flaws and weaknesses reflects acceptance of them for who they are, rather than what one wishes them to be. The genuine acceptance of one's partner, despite their failings and weaknesses, is one of the deepest expressions of caring and love.

Fairness clearly is an essential need in the success of a long-term relationship. The security and stability of a quality relationship rely on a reasonable balance of fairness and acceptance. This includes the ability to accept certain undesirable qualities and circumstances. Achieving a healthy balance of fairness and acceptance in a relationship is best accomplished through an attitude of generosity and caring. Establishing and maintaining fairness in a relationship conveys a deep level of caring, which serves as a foundation for a quality, stable, and long-lasting intimate relationship.

15

TEAMWORK
MAKING THE DREAM WORK

One of the hallmarks of a quality relationship is the ability to work as a team. An effective relationship team makes life much easier, more efficient, and reduces the overall stress load on a relationship. However, teamwork can be challenging for many couples. Each partner ideally comes from a different family background, so it should not be surprising that they may have significant differences in their beliefs about what a relationship should be and how it should function. Effectively working as a team is essential for blending each partner's potentially different approach to managing the everyday needs and responsibilities of their relationship. For these reasons, teamwork is an important need in the Green Zone.

Many couples are effective at managing everyday issues in their relationship but still may struggle with more significant problems. Although they can handle routine challenges with ease, they often find it difficult to work cooperatively when faced with more emotionally stressful situations. Problems that may be simple to solve individually can become much more difficult when working with a partner, as differing perspectives may not be easily aligned. Creating and building a successful relationship team is essential to the long-term quality and health of a relationship. Understanding the basic factors involved in relationship team building is essential for successfully managing challenging issues in an intimate relationship.

The first step in building a strong relationship team is to define what makes an effective team. A successful relationship team is a cooperative partnership between two partners, focused on creating a stable and satisfying relationship that builds relationship wealth over time.

The primary goal of teamwork in an intimate relationship is to meet the needs of both individuals as well as the needs of the relationship itself. Successfully addressing these needs greatly increases the likelihood of having a positive, satisfying, and stable relationship. In a successful relationship team, each partner is responsible for meeting their own needs, supporting their partner's needs, and working together to meet the needs of the relationship.

Benefits Of Teamwork

Working together as a team offers many benefits. One of the most significant is the reduction and prevention of relationship conflicts. The primary reason is that agreements made as a team are a kind of commitment, and much more likely to be durable and consistently followed by both partners.

Another benefit of teamwork is that many relationship problems can be challenging and require thoughtful and innovative solutions. Working together as a team, is more likely to lead to more intelligent solutions to solving problems and meeting relationship needs. Couples who work well together are more likely to find timely and effective solutions to their problems. In this regard, two heads are clearly better than one.

Another significant benefit of teamwork is that couples can complete everyday chores and responsibilities more efficiently when they work together. This increased efficiency saves both time and effort, allowing more opportunities for more enjoyable activities. Additionally, one partner may be better at managing or completing certain tasks, making it more practical to perform those responsibilities. The other partner may be better at certain other tasks. In this way, each partner contributes to meeting the needs of the relationship.

Another significant benefit of teamwork is financial. Having two incomes naturally increases financial resources. Sharing financial resources and expenses generally can reduce the financial burdens of each partner in the relationship, which otherwise could be a source of conflict in some relationships.

Finally, teamwork can provide protective benefits to a relationship by reducing overall stress. Couples who work effectively together develop a sense of unity, feel closer to each other, and generally experience greater relationship esteem and satisfaction.

There are clearly many significant benefits afforded to couples that work together as a team. Each of these advantages contributes to the overall level of relationship wealth that contributes to a healthy and durable relationship. As a result, couples who work well as a team have a distinct advantage over those who do not when addressing problems, both big and small.

Teamwork Benefits

- Better able to meet needs
- Improved relationship quality
- Relationship stability
- Prevention of conflict
- More intelligent solutions
- Able to manage greater work loads
- Increased efficiency
- Faster results
- More free time
- Greater fairness
- More resources
- Financial benefits
- Less stressful

- Protective benefit
- Sense of unity
- Greater relationship satisfaction

Relationship Team Characteristics

A successful relationship team is characterized by several important traits. Many needs that support a thriving relationship also are essential for an effective relationship team. For instance, shared leadership helps couples make better decisions when dealing with problems and challenges. This creates a sense of unity and equality between the partners. This collaborative approach allows them to better define common goals and establish clear expectations regarding the relationship and each other's needs.

Another key characteristic of a successful relationship team is effective communication. Couples need to be able to discuss their problems and needs openly. Achieving this requires a freedom of expression that allows each partner to discuss their needs openly without feeling fear, anxiety, or concern about the other partner's reaction.

One of the most important qualities of a successful relationship team is maintaining a positive team attitude. This is reflected in each partner's communication and behavior, which reinforces their identity as a team. A strong team attitude conveys respect, acceptance, tolerance, kindness, compassion, and genuine care for each other.

The team concept is based on the belief that relationships work best when two partners cooperate and work together rather than act independently. The emphasis shifts from "you" or "I" to "we" or "us." Placing the "team's" needs ahead of one's own needs is an important characteristic of successful couples.

A successful team perspective views relationship success as one based on interdependence and cooperation where both partners take active responsibility for the health and well-being of the relationship. Real (2022) provides a toolkit for helping couples move from self-focused thinking toward a collaborative and interdependent mindset that allows intimacy to grow through teamwork and mutual support.

Successful relationships commonly prioritize both relationship needs and individual needs. This can be challenging for many individuals if they have learned to focus primarily on their own needs throughout life and have limited experience in considering the needs of others. A team approach emphasizes the importance of both individual and relationship needs and is based on the idea that each partner's needs, and the needs of the relationship, are more effectively met within a team framework.

Building a relationship team requires the ability to compromise. This involves reaching agreements that serve the best interests of the relationship, rather than benefiting only one partner. A key factor in successful compromise is the willingness to make sacrifices. Often, this means being ready to sacrifice one's time, point of view, and personal desires to achieve the best outcome for the relationship.

Building A Successful Relationship Team

Building a strong relationship team is essential in developing and maintaining a high-quality, long-term relationship. This process requires consistent effort over time and must adapt to the changing needs of the relationship. While this commitment demands work, the benefits of teamwork are far greater than the work, stress, and conflict that often arise without it.

One of the most important elements in building an effective relationship team is creating a team identity. This identity is based in a shared belief that both partners view themselves as more than just individuals. This view creates a sense of "We" when addressing issues and making important decisions regarding the relationship.

The next step involves identifying the needs and responsibilities that need to be managed as a team. During this phase, each partner's needs and responsibilities are clearly defined. Next, the partners must agree on how these responsibilities will be handled. Finally, goals will be outlined to create a structured teamwork plan.

A primary function of teamwork is to establish agreements that address each partner's needs. All relationship responsibilities require some form of agreement. Given the numerous responsibilities involved, multiple agreements may be necessary to fulfill these needs. Determining which partner will do what and when can be challenging, making these agreements essential for providing a structured approach to meeting needs. The essential purpose of establishing team agreements is to make life simpler and more efficient. These agreements serve a critical role in saving time, simplifying responsibilities, and ultimately reducing stress. Healthy relationships thrive when stress is effectively kept at lower levels.

Once agreements have been established, they can be put to the test in everyday life. It is important, however, to expect that each agreement may require revisions and adjustments over time. It is essential that each agreement be flexible because relationship needs frequently change. As life changes, so may the need to modify agreements so that they remain fair and effective.

Common Team Agreements

There are many types of agreements that contribute to establishing a successful relationship. These may include the best approach for addressing problems, managing time and finances, dividing household chores, handling work responsibilities, parenting issues, and maintaining social relationships, among others. Each team agreement should be judged based on how effectively it supports the long-term needs of the relationship. Examples of effective team agreements can be found in Appendix C.

One of the most important team agreements is deciding when and how to discuss problems, needs, and other significant issues. For many couples, finding the right time and place to address relationship concerns can be challenging. Setting aside a specific time each week to focus on team needs is essential. Additionally, having a backup time is wise because distractions and unexpected circumstances can often interfere with this need. Having a specific time and place to discuss relationship issues is important because, generally, most other times are not suitable. Unfortunately, many couples try to force discussions at the worst possible times, such as when one is at work, heading out the door, when the children are around, or at bedtime.

For most busy couples, finding the right time to address issues can seem almost impossible. For this reason, having a dedicated time is essential for the success of the team. Setting aside dedicated time to discuss relationship issues helps couples develop a more balanced and comprehensive team approach. This strategy leads to better solutions that benefit the team, rather than favoring one partner over the other.

Most couples face similar types of issues in their relationship. Agreements need to be made regarding managing money, parenting, how time is spent, and how resources will be shared. Many of these agreements will be unique to each couple and will be based on their specific abilities and needs. These individualized agreements are necessary due to the potential differences between partners regarding family background, language, culture, life experiences, and expectations.

Most couples will deal with similar types of issues in their relationship, such as managing money, parenting, how time is spent, and how resources will be shared. However, what makes these discussions so challenging is the limited amount of time available for many couples.

One of the most important agreements for couples to make involves managing finances. This aspect of a relationship is often challenging and requires extensive discussion and planning. Several elements need to be addressed as part of this process, including how money will be spent, how much will be saved, whether to have joint or individual accounts, and what portion of income will go to nonessential expenses. Each of these areas can potentially lead to conflict and, therefore, require careful consideration.

Another common area requiring agreement is the management of chores and responsibilities. Someone must take out the garbage, wash clothes, handle shopping, mow the lawn, prepare meals, and clean the house. Without a satisfactory agreement, these tasks can quickly accumulate and become a source of conflict.

Parenting responsibilities often serve as another source of conflict for many couples. Questions arise regarding who will change diapers, give baths, or drive the kids to activities. Each of these areas has the potential to create conflict and stress. The more clearly defined an agreement is, the more effectively a couple can manage these issues.

Another common area that requires team agreement is managing relationships with extended family and friends. How often will you see family or friends? How will holidays and vacations be handled? When is it appropriate to give gifts? What are the priorities in terms of family, friends, and the couple's relationship? Each of these areas needs to be clarified to establish harmony and avoid potential problems.

Finding a balance between work and family needs is often a challenge for many couples. Work schedules, irregular hours, and weekend shifts can conflict with personal and family needs and obligations. Finding ways to meet all these needs in a balanced and satisfying way is an ongoing challenge for most couples.

Over time, most couples will develop agreements that work effectively for them. Some of these agreements may be very simple ones, such as determining who does the dishes, while others may be more complex and present greater challenges to successfully maintain.

Problems and disagreements are a natural part of all relationships. What determines a couple's success is how effectively they function as a team in creating agreements that meet both their individual needs and relationship needs. The more a couple focuses on achieving this goal, the more stable and positive their relationship will become.

Finally, it is important to keep in mind that teamwork is an ongoing process that requires regular maintenance. Once the major team agreements have been established, the focus shifts to maintaining those agreements. Agreements that were effective in the past may need to be revised to adapt to new conditions.

The most successful couples have learned to work together effectively as a team to define and establish agreements for managing their needs and responsibilities. As a result, they function more efficiently, save time, and reduce stress in their relationship. The time and effort invested in creating strong team agreements is a vital and valuable investment in an intimate relationship. This effort of working together as a team contributes to building relationship wealth, which leads to achieving a successful and satisfying long-term relationship.

16

COMMITMENT
THE POWER OF PROMISE

One of the most important needs of a successful relationship is commitment. It is impossible to sustain a high-quality relationship without a level of commitment. Relationships undergo numerous challenges that require commitment to endure the stress associated with these challenges. For this reason, commitment is an essential need in the Green Zone.

Commitment can be defined as an agreement or pledge to devote oneself to another person. It consists of a promise or assurance to remain dedicated to a partner in both good times and bad. Devoting one's life to another person is one of the most significant decisions one can make in life. The ability to commit oneself to the common mission of building and maintaining a long-term relationship requires a significant personal sacrifice.

Commitment is essentially an agreement between both partners to devote themselves to the needs of each other and of their relationship. This agreement is reinforced through the deliberate and consistent efforts each partner makes to uphold their promise to each other. Commitment is, in essence, an agreement that promises devotion to the relationship. It involves a plan of action to consistently commit one's time, energy, and other resources toward building relationship wealth and maintaining a healthy long-term relationship.

Commitment to a lifelong relationship requires a belief that the relationship is right for both partners, meets their personal needs, and is worth the sacrifices involved. The decision to commit to a relationship should be based not only on feelings but also on how well the relationship meets each partner's definition of what constitutes a meaningful relationship.

Strong relationships are built on dedication involving a conscious decision to invest in long-term commitment. One viewpoint is that commitment should be based on a clear desire or choice as opposed to one based on external factors such as kids or finances. (Markman, et.al. 2024). In essence, a couple may slide into a deeper level of commitment because of external factors rather than do so because of a clear and genuine desire for commitment.

The decision to commit to a long-term relationship is significantly influenced by emotions. These emotions often provide an essential energy that supports commitment.

However, the unstable nature of emotions is a primary reason why relationships can be inherently unstable. Emotions can greatly affect the level of commitment that partners have to each other. Because emotions often change over time, it is important that a commitment be based not only on emotional factors but also on whether a relationship makes rational sense.

Commitment, in essence, rests on the core belief that a relationship holds significant and meaningful value, making it worth the effort and dedication required. Without a rational belief or conviction that the relationship is one that is worth committing to, emotional factors can undermine a commitment and impact the stability and quality needed to maintain a long-term relationship.

The Benefits of Commitment

Commitment offers many important advantages in a long-term intimate relationship. One of the primary benefits is relationship stability. Commitment provides a stable foundation upon which a long-term relationship can be built. Therefore, as mentioned earlier, it is essential for commitment to be based on rational factors which both support and reinforce the emotions that drive an intimate relationship.

Another key benefit of commitment is emotional security. When one partner believes they can depend on the other partner, especially during difficult times, the couple is likely to experience a greater sense of emotional security within the relationship.

Commitment can also be seen as a significant expression of caring. When one partner commits to another, they are making a statement that they recognize the other's great value and meaning by choosing to invest their life with them. There is perhaps nothing more meaningful than one partner dedicating their life and future to another. Since a person's self-worth may be partly influenced by how others perceive them, commitment can have a positive impact on their self-esteem.

Another significant advantage of commitment is that it reduces overall stress in a relationship. When a couple is committed to each other, they can share the burden of stress more easily, making it easier to cope with the challenges in an intimate relationship. Having a supportive and committed partner enhances one's ability to manage life's responsibilities more effectively.

Finally, commitment in a relationship provides additional resources for addressing both individual and shared needs. The combined resources of two partners can significantly increase overall quality of life, as there is often more time, financial stability, and energy available to meet the demands of the relationship.

The Commitment Decision

The decision to commit one's life to a long-term relationship involves several important factors. It takes time and patience to determine if such a commitment will truly meet one's needs. Since emotional factors play a significant role in this the decision, there is often a tendency to commit too soon, which can lead to later regrets.

The decision to make a commitment to a long-term intimate relationship involves both rational and emotional factors, with love being the most common emotional factor. Partners often choose to commit to each other out of love and a desire to share their lives together. Without love and other positive emotions, building and maintaining a meaningful long-term relationship would be difficult.

Although love is an essential factor in an intimate relationship, it is also one of the most blinding. Many people decide to commit to a relationship based solely on love, only to realize later that it was a mistake for one or both partners. Love and other positive emotions often exaggerate or distort one's perceptions and expectations. These positive feelings can be intoxicating, leading individuals to overlook negative factors that might otherwise cause them to delay or refuse commitment.

In addition to love, several other emotional factors influence the decision to commit to a relationship. For example, sexual feelings can lead people to commit to a relationship prematurely, even when there are clear reasons to avoid commitment. These intense sexual feelings can distort judgment and create unrealistic expectations regarding commitment.

The desire to commit to a partner is also influenced by how emotionally secure one feels in the relationship. A long-term commitment requires a solid foundation of security. Any factor that makes one partner feel insecure is likely to undermine the commitment decision. This is why it is so important for couples to explore and address any issue that may be a source of insecurity prior to making any commitment.

Essentially, feelings of love, happiness, and sexual pleasure play a significant role in the decision to commit to an intimate relationship. Each of these emotions contributes to how willing one is to commit to a long-term relationship. As a result, the level of desire for commitment generally is based primarily on emotional factors.

On the other hand, negative emotions can also significantly affect the decision to make a commitment. For instance, the fear of being alone can lead one into a commitment that may not be in their best interest. Many people are willing to make unwise commitments just to avoid being alone, even if the relationship is not the right fit or doesn't meet their needs.

Other negative emotions can also play a significant role in why people choose not to commit to a long-term relationship. For example, frequent expressions of anger, criticism, or negativity can greatly reduce the desire to commit to a relationship with someone.

The primary risk of commitment based solely on emotions is that the relationship will rest on an unstable foundation, as emotions can change dramatically over time. In such cases, commitment becomes as unstable as the emotions experienced on any given day. Since most relationships go through periods of emotional distress, the relationship would be vulnerable during these times, with increased anxiety and tension likely to impact the level of commitment. Therefore, it is essential that the commitment decision be based on rational factors that align with one's values, needs, and long-term goals.

Emotional factors alone can significantly influence the decision to commit. It is essential to also clearly define rational factors that could have an impact as well. One of the most important rational factors is the ability to communicate about relationship needs and problems. Effective communication is key to building and sustaining a healthy relationship. Without it, meeting the needs of the relationship becomes impossible.

Another important quality for maintaining commitment is dependability. Long-term commitment requires both partners to believe that they can rely on each other, particularly during times of stress. A couple that trusts in each other's dependability, both in good times and bad, will experience a much stronger level of commitment to their relationship.

The decision to commit to a long-term relationship is closely linked to the level of compatibility between partners. Couples who share similar backgrounds, values, and interests are more likely to commit to one another and to sustain a lasting commitment.

The relationship between compatibility and commitment is important for the stability of a long-term relationship. Sharing common interests, for example, increases both the quantity and quality of time a couple spends together. As a result, they have more activities to enjoy, more shared experiences, and more to talk about.

Compatibility plays a significant role in various aspects of a stable relationship. One important aspect is family values, which can include decisions about having children, relationships with extended family and friends, and the amount of much time spent with others outside of the relationship.

Another area of compatibility relates to the type of lifestyle desired. For instance, one partner may value a healthy lifestyle that includes regular exercise and good nutrition, while the other may have little interest in fitness and may indulge in excessive eating or alcohol consumption.

Compatibility can also impact affection and sexual needs. Frequently, one partner may have a greater desire for affection or sexual intimacy than the other. Significant differences in this area are a common source of conflict for many couples. This issue can be particularly challenging because many partners find it difficult to communicate their needs for affection and sexual intimacy to their partner.

Compatibility in financial matters is another crucial area where values should align. For instance, one partner may be frugal and want to save every penny, while the other may spend impulsively without concern for the consequences. Additionally, one partner may prefer to combine financial resources, while the other may prefer to maintain separate accounts.

Other important aspects of compatibility include religious beliefs, cultural values, and even political views. Each of these areas can significantly influence the commitment decision. Therefore, it is important for partners to discuss these areas prior to commitment in order to ensure that they have a clear understanding of each other's needs.

Given the wide range of potential differences between partners, there are likely to be several areas of incompatibility. However, it is not just the number of differences that matters but, more importantly, the significance of those differences. The greater the incompatibility, the more stress that will likely be placed on the relationship.

Ultimately, the foundation of commitment rests on all the sixteen-core relationship needs, with each serving as a pillar that supports a successful relationship. A weakness in one area can affect the stability of the others. Therefore, the decision to commit to a long-term relationship should always be based on solid rational factors, rather than on emotions only.

Factors in the Commitment Decision

Emotional Factors

- Love
- Emotional security
- Sexual feelings
- Happiness
- Pleasure
- Fear
- Loneliness

Rational Factors

- Communication
- Ability to solve problems
- Loyalty
- Trust
- Honesty
- Dependability
- Compatibility – Interests, finances, family / social relationships

Commitment Avoidance

Just as love and other positive emotions can influence the decision to commit to a relationship, negative feelings can also play a role in such decisions. Anxiety, insecurity, frustration, and similar emotions may prevent someone from making a commitment. These feelings often reflect valid concerns about the quality or longevity of the relationship. While mixed emotions are a normal part of many relationships, there are times when they stem from realistic concerns.

While negative emotions play an important role in the commitment decision, the absence of positive emotions is equally significant. If one's feelings about a partner lack a satisfying level of positive feelings, it suggests that commitment may not be the best choice.

It is important to remember that commitment is not always absolute. The level of commitment in a relationship can vary, ranging from total commitment to partial or conditional commitment, or even to one where genuine commitment is lacking.

The decision to commit to a long-term relationship generally evolves over time, particularly in the early stages as feelings grow and areas of compatibility are explored. As both partners get to know each other and their feelings deepen, the question of commitment naturally arises. The process unfolds at a different pace for each partner, based on personalities and the interactions between them.

True commitment requires that one feel secure in the belief that the other partner can meet one's needs in a long-term relationship. Without this confidence, the level of commitment is likely to be much more limited. However, developing this sense of security can take time.

The avoidance of commitment can be due to various factors. One significant factor may be negative feelings from past relationships. For instance, if someone has experienced a painful breakup, they may have unresolved feelings about the breakup that prevent them from committing to a new relationship. Issues such as past infidelity or problems with trust can also make a partner reluctant to fully commit in a new relationship.

In some cases, commitment may be avoided because one partner needs time to resolve feelings from a past relationship. Additionally, challenges related to significant geographic distances, career or educational demands, or other reasons may contribute to a reluctance to commit. In other instances, the avoidance of commitment may be due to difficulty accepting certain traits or qualities in the partner.

Commitment is generally not an all-or-nothing decision, especially in the beginning of a relationship. It often depends on various conflicting factors that can make it difficult to fully commit to a long-term relationship. A partner may be committed in most areas, but not all areas. For instance, a partner may be willing to invest a significant amount of time in the relationship but be less willing to share finances or participate in family events. In this case, such commitment is essentially partial.

Partial commitments often lead to significant emotional distress, as they create sense of unfairness in the relationship. If these specific "trouble" areas of commitment are not resolved, the relationship is likely to remain emotionally stressful and unstable.

Another form of commitment is conditional. In this case, one partner may express a desire for commitment, but only under certain conditions. A conditional commitment involves a willingness to commit, but only if certain conditions or needs are met. For example, one partner may be willing to commit, but only if they do not have to invest much time, effort, or work in the relationship. In other cases, the conditions may be based on the other partner's willingness to relocate, change religion, or gives up their friends.

Both conditional and partial commitments are common sources of conflict and distress in relationships. These types of commitment are often found in distressed relationships and, as a result, frequently lead to relationship stress and failure.

In healthy long-term relationships, genuine commitment is neither conditional nor partial. Instead, it is a lifelong dedication to both partner's needs and to the needs of the relationship itself. This commitment is grounded in the belief that both emotional and rational factors are aligned with each partner's values and goals.

In practice, maintaining a quality relationship requires a substantial commitment of time, effort, and dedication. Couples in successful relationships are motivated to invest their resources into building and sustaining a healthy and stable relationship. They devote themselves to building relationship wealth and prioritizing each other and meeting the needs of the relationship. While commitment does require work and sacrifice, the benefits far outweigh the costs. The greatest reward is the satisfaction and fulfillment that comes from a strong, lasting relationship.

17

FRIENDSHIP

MORE THAN SHARED EXPERIENCES

F riendship plays a major role in the success of long-term relationships. When a relationship is based on a genuine friendship, the friendship greatly contributes to the relationship's overall health and longevity. In fact, friendship is often considered to be one of the strongest predictors of longevity in intimate relationships. Friendship, therefore, is an important need in the Green Zone.

Friendship generally can be defined as a bond or relationship with another person, based on shared feelings, beliefs, or activities that provide pleasure or satisfaction. Friendship can exist in many types of relationships besides those with an intimate partner, such as those with peers, family members, coworkers, neighbors, and others.

The focus here is on friendship in an intimate relationship. In this context, friendship is much more extensive and involved than in other types of relationships. It includes sharing a wider range of activities and experiences, many of them intimate, over a longer period of time. This form of friendship is also more challenging because it involves sharing both positive and negative experiences together. Activities such as managing chores, coping with stress, and handling everyday demands of life are typically not shared in other types of friendships.

Most friendships involve spending limited time together compared to the friendship time shared in an intimate relationship. The stakes are higher, and the challenges are much greater when you are spending time with someone day and night, as opposed to spending only brief periods of time together.

"General" friendships typically revolve around specific activities, such as having lunch, playing golf, exercising, or work-related activities. These friendships often have a narrow focus, concentrating on particular interests or activities. In contrast, intimate relationships involve a broader range of activities over an extended period.

The benefits of being in an intimate relationship based on friendship are numerous. One of the most significant advantages of this type of friendship is the sense of security and trust it fosters. Couples connected through shared interests and activities generally experience a higher level of security and trust in their relationship. Additionally, the quality of the bond in an intimate relationship is often stronger and more satisfying than that found in a typical non-intimate friendship.

Another important benefit of a friendship-based intimate relationship is better communication. Because the relationship spans a wider range of life activities, there is generally more to be engaged with and talk about. In essence, friendship in an intimate relationship combines multiple common interests and shared goals with a deeper overall emotional connection.

Another advantage of friendship in an intimate relationship is that it reinforces commitment to solving problems and managing stress together. This aspect of friendship contributes to a greater willingness to listen, seek understanding, and promote mutual respect. It also encourages partners to work together as a team to meet relationship needs, achieve goals, and address challenges as they arise.

Couples in successful long-term relationships are not only intimate partners but also friends who genuinely care for each other. They cultivate and maintain a connection with each other on multiple levels, sharing interests, activities, family relationships, and similar values. Additionally, they have a mutual desire to express nurturance, affection, and physical passion that is satisfying to both.

On the other hand, couples in distressed relationships often prioritize their own needs and interests over those of their partners. They frequently judge the relationship based on how well it satisfies their own individual desires. As a result, they tend to be less generous in their interactions compared to couples who share a strong friendship.

When a couple's relationship is built on friendship, it enhances both the longevity and quality of their bond. A friendship-based relationship reinforces a deeper level of companionship, understanding, and respect. Partners see each other not only as companions but also as allies, working together toward the shared goal of creating a meaningful life.

Friendship with an intimate partner can, in many respects, resemble other types of friendship. However, there are some significant differences. One of the primary distinctions is physical and sexual intimacy, which serves as a unique and pleasurable source of connection that strengthens the bond between partners. Additionally, the way that intimate partners communicate and interact with each other differs from how they relate to others in other friendships. For example, intimate partners often express their love verbally, plan date nights, send love notes, and engage in other romantic gestures.

In successful intimate relationships, love and friendship are deeply intertwined. Friendship can lead to feelings of affection, passion, and love, which can deepen the relationship and friendship bond. Each experience often strengthens the other, creating a dynamic connection between the two. This interplay between love and friendship reinforces the bond between intimate partners.

One reason that intimate relationships grounded in friendship tend to be more successful is that couples in this category are generally much more open and relaxed with each other. They experience a greater degree of security and comfort, which allows them to reveal more about themselves and their desires. Additionally, there is also a greater degree of generosity in sharing resources, time, and emotional support.

Another part of any great friendship is having shared interests. Engaging in similar activities and hobbies enhances the quality of a relationship in many ways. Intimate friendships are more easily sustained when they involve shared hobbies, work tasks, intellectual interests, and other activities that provide mutual enjoyment. Having interests that both partners find satisfying enriches the time they spend together. These shared experiences become a major source of positive emotional fulfillment, increasing the overall satisfaction in the relationship.

Friendship plays a major role in building relationship wealth. Sharing life with a loving partner on emotional, social, intellectual, and physical levels creates a deeply positive experience that strengthens the overall health of an intimate friendship.

Building Friendship in an Intimate Relationship

Building friendship in an intimate relationship requires time and effort. By understanding each other's needs, desires, and interests, the friendship can grow deeper. This process involves focusing on quality communication, developing shared interests, and seeking mutually desired activities. Nurturing a quality friendship enhances the overall quality and richness of the relationship. Though cultivating friendship requires an investment of additional time and effort, the returns are significant, leading to greater stability and quality in the partnership.

There are many ways in which friendship plays a role in the health of intimate relationships. One of the most important factors to remember is that friendship is built on the many small things that couples say and do with each other. It is the daily routine actions that are the bedrock of intimate friendship. Feldhahn (2013) provides a practical, research-based guide focused on the daily behaviors that build and strengthen friendship and commitment in intimate relationships.

Cultivating friendship involves exploring new activities and experiences together. This allows one to determine where there are common interests to build a friendship upon. Uncovering each other's likes and dislikes, interests, goals, philosophy of life, and even quirks, serves as an opportunity to build the elements of friendship by which an additional meaningful connection can be developed within the intimate relationship.

Finding mutually interesting subjects to discuss is important for all couples. The wider the range of shared subjects and interests, the more satisfying and stable a relationship is likely to be. However, not all interests will hold the same value or appeal to both partners equally. It is important to regularly explore new ideas and activities as a couple, which helps keep the relationship fresh and vibrant by introducing new sources of positive emotional fulfillment.

Many couples fall into the habit of discussing only everyday issues and problems, which can make their conversations feel bland and unsatisfying. When the pleasure of conversation fades, it can start to drain the relationship and weaken the friendship. Introducing new activities and experiences, therefore, plays an important role in maintaining the long-term health of the relationship.

One of the important activities that successful couples engage in to reinforce their friendship is to plan regular date nights. For many couples this involves finding a day each week where they can get away from daily routines and responsibilities so that they can prioritize their intimate connection. It offers an opportunity to recharge the relationship's energy and reinforce the shared goals that make the relationship meaningful.

Date nights also provide an opportunity to spend time together in a new environment. When planning a date night, it is helpful to try different things rather than always doing the same thing. A good strategy is for partners to alternate as to who will chooses the activity each week, ensuring a steady flow of fresh experiences.

Activities that reinforce friendship may not always align with both partner's interests. It is natural for couples to have different hobbies or activities that one partner may not enjoy. However, it is important to try to support each other's interests for personal growth and fulfillment. Generally, if one partner is passionate about a particular hobby or interest, it can be beneficial for the other partner to find ways to participate or show interest in the activity when possible.

Building friendship in a relationship takes time and requires a consistent day-to-day process. However, the time invested in cultivating friendship is important to the long-term health and quality of an intimate relationship. Nurturing a lifelong friendship greatly enhances the quality of a shared partnership. The main point to remember is that one partner is not just sharing life with another but also sharing a friendship with that partner for life. Over time, the process of building a friendship with an intimate partner is a primary factor in building relationship wealth and enjoying a lifelong satisfying bond with another.

THE YELLOW ZONE

18

SOLVING RELATIONSHIP PROBLEMS
TURNING STUMBLING BLOCKS INTO STEPPING STONES

All couples will, at one time or another, experience relationship problems. Problems and conflicts are a natural part of relationships, particularly intimate ones. Throughout the course of a relationship, numerous challenges will arise. The ability to manage these issues is essential for ensuring the long-term health and stability of the relationship. Maintaining a healthy partnership relies on the ability to prevent, reduce, or resolve problems that cause relationship stress.

When a couple addresses problems or needs in their relationship they are in the Yellow Zone, or problem-solving phase. This phase is emotionally challenging because it requires both effective problem-solving skills and the ability to manage emotional reactions that arise from relationship conflicts. Successfully navigating this combination of factors is critical for the long-term health and stability of an intimate relationship.

Building relationship wealth requires the knowledge, ability, and skills to effectively manage and resolve the many problems experienced in a relationship over time. By their nature, relationship problems can be frustrating and emotionally stressful. Often, the emotional reactions associated with problems can be a greater challenge to the relationship than the problems themselves. Most relationship problems tend to be small, everyday issues that generally cause relatively minor stress. However, there will also be more challenging problems that are emotionally stressful and difficult to solve. These larger problems can test the strength and resilience of a relationship. Ultimately, the ability to successfully address relationship problems effectively will play a major role in the success or failure of the relationship.

Generally, there are two major groups of problems. Those that are solvable and those that are perpetual or adaptive. Gottman, (2015) found that an average of 69% of conflicts that couples experience are perpetual problems that are rooted in basic differences between partners. As a result, couples must find a way to adapt, compromise, and accept these differences if they are to maintain health and stability in their relationships.

The ability to solve relationship problems is generally independent of how strong the emotional bond of the relationship is. While love and other positive emotions may help buffer the effects of stress, they do little to resolve problems. Conflicts in a relationship can create intense negative emotions like anger, resentment, and anxiety, which can disrupt positive feelings such as love and happiness. Unfortunately, many couples in distressed relationships lack the skills to manage their emotional responses effectively. For this reason, it is essential for couples to learn how to successfully manage problems to protect their relationship from the damaging impact of these negative emotions.

All couples will experience problems and stress in their relationship as it grows and evolves over time. This is a normal part of any intimate relationship. It does not mean that a relationship is failing, or that love is lacking. By successfully navigating challenging problems, a relationship can become stronger and more resilient as it matures. In fact, working through problems together can lead to a deeper level of intimacy between partners.

Couples in distressed relationships often believe that their relationship is struggling or failing because of the problems they have.

However, it is generally not the problems themselves that are the primary issue. Instead, it is most often the approach to solving problems that is the real issue. Couples using the wrong approach to problem solving are much more likely to struggle or fail, regardless of the nature of the problem. With the wrong approach, even minor problems can become overwhelming and seem impossible to resolve.

A negative approach to problem-solving often triggers negative emotional reactions, which can weaken the ability to resolve relationship problems. Emotions like frustration, anger, resentment, and anxiety make the problem-solving process much more difficult and can significantly increase stress on a relationship.

Many couples in distressed relationships spend countless hours struggling with problems, often the same ones, which can add up to thousands of hours over the course of their relationship. The emotional toll this takes on each partner and the relationship is enormous. However, couples who learn to adopt a more effective team-based approach can significantly reduce the time and stress associated with managing their problems. The goal of this approach is to improve a couple's ability to resolve problems more effectively and to eliminate the cycle of arguing and fighting.

To successfully manage relationship problems, effective communication is essential, but it also requires a specific approach to addressing challenging issues. This approach involves identifying and defining the problem, negotiating and agreeing on the best strategy, and then implementing the proposed solution. All of this must be done while managing strong emotional reactions, which can make the issues feel overwhelming and unsolvable.

Effectively resolving problems in a relationship offers numerous benefits. One of the most important is a substantial reduction in stress. Essentially, the better a couple is at solving their relationship problems, the less emotional strain they will experience. This reduced burden creates an environment where positive emotions can flourish more easily. Other important benefits include increased relationship stability, better satisfaction of needs, increased relationship esteem, greater intimacy, and ultimately, a healthier, more satisfying relationship.

Successful vs. Distressed Relationships

There are major differences in how successful and distressed couples approach relationship problems. These differences significantly impact how effectively a couple can resolve problems, and consequently, plays a crucial role in determining the overall success or failure of the relationship.

Couples in successful relationships consistently take a team approach to addressing their problems. Their primary goal is to meet each other's needs, find solutions to their problems, and prevent emotional reactions from harming their relationship. They are also mindful that differences in viewpoint, potential misunderstandings, and emotional reactions can influence and disrupt this process.

Successful couples strive to achieve clarity in their understanding of problems, while trying to prevent or correct any misunderstanding. They communicate in a way that progressively moves their understanding toward greater clarity. There is a significant emphasis on gaining a clear understanding of the problem, without which the chance of resolving a problem is greatly diminished.

Individuals in successful relationships understand the importance of resolving problems while managing their emotions. This contrasts with couples in distressed relationships, who are much more easily emotionally triggered and lose focus on their shared goal of resolving problems together. Developing the ability to manage emotions will be further addressed in the next chapter.

Distressed couples also tend to take a more emotionally negative approach to addressing problems. Their interactions are often characterized by poor listening and negative communication, especially when emotions run high. Rather than working together, they focus more on their own perspective than on their partner's perspective. They frequently interrupt, cut each other off, dismiss each other's viewpoints, or try to undermine or belittle their partner's words and feelings. They are also more likely to be uncooperative, oppositional, and competitive in handling relationship issues. As a result, misunderstandings between the partners are more frequent and more severe.

Successful couples prioritize gaining an accurate understanding of a problem. They often ask questions to clarify the issue and avoid misunderstandings. In contrast, distressed couples tend to ask fewer questions and are more likely to make assumptions or jump to premature conclusions. As a result, they are far less effective at establishing a clear understanding of the problem. Distressed couples also tend to focus more on their differences and areas of disagreement than on points of agreement. They often resort to avoidance and procrastination when dealing with relationship issues. As a result, problems remain unsolved, needs go unmet, and stress becomes a chronic problem in the relationship.

Distressed couples are more likely to struggle with managing anger and frustration, often resorting to attacking or blaming each other for problems that arise. Additionally, they tend to find it difficult to apologize or take responsibility for their actions when they are at fault.

Couples in distressed relationships not only spend more time in conflict with each other they also tend to dwell on negative thoughts and feelings about their problems when they are apart. The focus on negativity, combined with frequent arguments, can lead to countless hours of stress over the course of the relationship. Such prolonged stress may exceed what many relationships can withstand.

Another key difference between successful and distressed couples is how they focus on multiple issues. Successful couples focus on one issue at a time and understand that it takes several conversations to find a good solution. In contrast, distressed couples tend to bring up multiple past issues during discussions, turning problem-solving into an overwhelming and unproductive effort.

Another characteristic of successful couples is their understanding that most problems stem from unmet needs within the relationship. By viewing problems in this way, they are more likely to take a positive approach to finding solutions. In contrast, distressed couples often focus on assigning blame for a problem rather than on identifying the underlying need or solution. They frequently see solutions as dependent on their partner changing their position or viewpoint rather than addressing the root cause of a problem together.

The goal in managing relationship problems is to agree on the best course of action. Successful couples work together to find solutions that address the issue and meet each partner's needs. In contrast, distressed couples often fail to reach agreements and remain trapped in a cycle of chronic disagreement, making it difficult for them to build a healthy and stable relationship.

Successful Relationships

Team communication
Cooperative attitude
Listen to understand
Motivated to address problems
Address problems in a timely manner
Positive focus
Maintain control over negative emotions
Focus on one problem at a time
Focused on facts
Able to reach successful agreements
Adaptive to ongoing problems

Distressed Relationships

Aggressive / avoidance pattern
Competitive / oppositional attitude
Poor listening
Unmotivated to address problems
Procrastinate or ignore problems
Negative focus on problems

Negative emotional reactions - Anger
Focus on multiple problems at once
Draw conclusions based on assumptions
Unable to reach or maintain agreements
Difficulty accepting differences

Managing Relationship Problems

Learning how to effectively resolve problems as a couple is essential for maintaining the long-term quality and stability of a relationship. Successfully managing relationship issues depends on a set of skills that helps couples to reach agreements that help to resolve problems and meet the needs of each partner and those of the relationship. One of the most important initial agreements is to establish a structured approach for addressing problems, including how, when, and where to discuss relationship challenges and needs.

Adopting a team approach that emphasizes mutual support and cooperative communication is an important goal for addressing issues as a couple. This approach helps set boundaries to ensure respect for each other's viewpoints. It also increases each partner's motivation to work together in finding positive solutions to their problems.

A positive team-oriented attitude allows couples to address relationship problems with a consistent and predictable approach to problems, whether it is some small issue or one that is more complex and challenging. Using the same approach to problems each time creates a more efficient process that results in a better understanding and better outcome for the partners and for the relationship.

Another important guideline in problem-solving is to address issues as soon as possible. Generally, it is more effective to discuss problems early. Waiting until they become urgent can lead to greater stress and make solving them much more difficult.

Many couples have limited time to address problems, which makes it essential to set aside adequate time for this important need. It is extremely helpful to have a predictable day and time to discuss relationship issues. While everyday issues can be resolved as they arise, more complex problems may require a significant amount of time to fully understand and address. For this reason, it is important to anticipate having multiple discussions to resolve them. In fact, most relationship problems require several meetings, depending on their complexity and emotional intensity. Generally, the more complicated or emotionally difficult an issue is, the more time that will be needed to resolve it.

For most couples, there are right and wrong times to address problems. The best time to discuss difficult issues is when both partners can give their full, undivided attention. Trying to resolve problems at the wrong time is more likely to result in misunderstandings and increased emotional stress. It is important to recognize that certain times are not ideal for these discussions, such as just before bedtime, while at work, upon arriving home or leaving, or when other pressing demands require attention.

A common issue to be considered is how long couples should spend discussing problems. Some prefer to limit the amount of time to prevent excessive stress, while others set no boundaries and may discuss problems endlessly. While it is important to allow enough time to make progress toward a resolution, marathon discussions can be draining and increase the risk of stress overload.

Another key guideline in problem-solving is to begin by focusing on areas of agreement regarding a problem before addressing more emotionally challenging points of disagreement. This approach helps to encourage positive communication, enhance listening, and establish a more cooperative mindset.

The Problem-Solving Process

Solving relationship problems can sometimes feel overwhelming. To make the process easier, it helps to break problems down into manageable segments or steps. This allows both partners to focus on one step at a time in a logical manner, rather than relying on an emotionally driven, scattered approach that can lead to frustration.

Each step in the problem-solving process serves a specific purpose. The first step is to identify and define the problem clearly so that both partners understand it. While some issues are straightforward, others may be more complex and harder to define. For example, one partner may feel that some aspect of the relationship is unfair, but clarification of exactly what that means requires further explanation. Gathering these details is essential for gaining the understanding necessary to explore potential solutions. It is important to examine when the problem occurs, how often, and most importantly, how it affects each partner and the relationship.

One way to gain a clearer understanding of a problem is by viewing it from three different perspectives. The first, and perhaps the easiest, is by an individual's own perspective. This viewpoint comes naturally and often occurs automatically, but it can also be biased in favor of one's own position.

The second perspective is that of one's partner. This requires the ability to see the issue from the other partner's point of view, while temporarily setting aside one's own perspective. It is easier to do this when there is agreement, but it becomes much more challenging in more complex situations where opinions differ.

Many people make the mistake of focusing only on their own point of view and fail to fully explore their partner's perspective. It is important to recognize that the other partner's viewpoint is also valid. The ability to consider and understand each other's perspective is essential to a team approach to relationship problem-solving and enables each partner to better understand what the other thinks, feels, and needs.

The third perspective is the team perspective. This involves evaluating the problem in terms of how it affects the relationship overall and its impact on the long-term health and stability of the relationship. This involves looking at problems based on a blend of the partners' viewpoints. This approach typically leads to the partners having a more comprehensive understanding of the issue.

Once the problem is clearly understood, the next step is to identify the underlying need that it represents. Framing a problem in terms of its underlying need is a more constructive approach, as it generally reduces blame and minimizes negative emotional reactions. This shift in focus serves to highlight the unmet needs within the relationship and emphasizes how those needs can be better addressed.

Identifying the underlying need associated with a problem can be challenging and is often not immediately obvious. For example, a couple might argue about who is responsible for certain chores, but the deeper issue could be a lack of fairness in the relationship. Once the true need is recognized, steps can be taken to address it directly, increasing the chances of a more positive and effective resolution.

Problems can often stem from a single need, such as a desire for more affection. However, many relationship issues and problems involve multiple needs. For example, when one partner expresses that they do not feel loved, it may not only reflect a desire for more love but also may involve other needs, such as a desire to spend more time together or a desire to be treated with greater respect. This subject can be so emotionally sensitive that it is essential for each partner to seek clarification by asking specific questions that can uncover the real question or issue.

At times, a problem may seem to be about one need but turn out to be about an entirely different one. For example, a couple might argue about trust, when the deeper issue is a need for greater security in the relationship. To accurately determine the underlying need or needs behind a problem, it is important to ask specific questions to identify the need involved.

Once the key needs behind a problem are accurately identified and understood, the next step is to explore all possible ways to address those needs. The more potential solutions that are identified, the better the chances of finding the right solutions. It is essential to discuss and negotiate the pros and cons of each option. Often, the best outcome is a combination of solutions that best fit the specific problem or need.

Once a couple agrees on the best solution to a problem, the next step is to implement the solution and evaluate its effectiveness. It is important to understand that potential solutions often take time to show results, so they should be given sufficient time to evolve before the partners consider any alternatives. During this phase, adjustments are typically necessary. In addition, unforeseen obstacles may arise, requiring modifications to the solution.

Finding the ideal solution to many relationship problems often involves adjustments, sacrifices and compromises. In some cases, there may be no perfect solution. When this happens, it may be necessary to accept a less-than-ideal option, one that causes the least amount of stress. Such solutions may rely more on sacrifice or acceptance than on achieving the ideal outcome. In these situations, couples need to agree on the best way to adapt or accept the reality of the situation. Developing the ability to adapt to problems that have no clear solution is a vital skill for all successful couples.

In some situations where resolving a conflict seems impossible, seeking outside consultation may be necessary to facilitate the resolution process. No couple should expect to have the solution to every issue they encounter. Preserving the quality, stability, and health of one's relationship is far too important to allow any issue or problem to become or remain a chronic source of harm to the relationship.

Problem-Solving Steps

- Definition / description of the problem
- Manage emotional reactions
- Identifying the needs underlying relationship problems
- Evaluating potential solutions
- Determining the best potential solution
- Implementation of the solution
- Determining if the solution works
- Evaluating if the solution can be improved

Common Relationship Problems

Relationship problems typically fall into several common categories, including communication, intimacy, emotional reactions, financial issues, household responsibilities, parenting, social relationships, time management, and health related behavior. Each of these areas are frequently associated with recurring conflicts, frustration, and general dissatisfaction in relationships.

One of the most frequent challenges for couples is with communication. As noted earlier, communication can profoundly influence a relationship, either positively or negatively. Effective communication strengthens the relationship and builds relationship wealth, while poor communication can significantly harm a relationship's quality, health, and stability.

Another common source of relationship problems is intimacy. Both emotional and physical intimacy can often lead to conflict or frustration, because they are deeply tied to each partner's need to feel loved. A lack of intimacy is frequently the underlying cause of many other problems in relationships.

For couples with children, parenting is often a source of stress that can affect the quality of their relationship. Disagreements over parenting styles and shared responsibilities are frequently sources of conflict and stress. Successfully working as a parenting team can be challenging and requires time in which to become skilled.

Family and other social relationship conflicts are a common source of problems in relationships. For many couples, time together is limited. As a result, anything that intrudes into that time can be a source of stress. These issues frequently occur around conflicts with time spent with others. It is not uncommon for these conflicts to be emotionally challenging because they are often perceived as one partner prioritizing the time spent with someone else over the needs of the relationship.

Another common source of conflict in relationships are financial issues. These problems often revolve around issues of not having enough money, disagreements over spending habits, or over who should manage the finances. Given that many individuals come from vastly different financial backgrounds, it is not surprising that conflicts often arise. When one partner is a spender and the other is a saver, conflicts are inevitable.

Many financial conflicts stem from the failure to establish a budget or financial plan that both partners perceive as fair and which meets their needs. Often, one or both partners must come to terms with the reality of the relationship's limited resources or adjust their financial expectations to align with their circumstances.

Sharing household chores and responsibilities is likely to be a source of stress for nearly every couple at some point. There are always ongoing tasks that need attention, many of which neither partner wants to do. This is one of the realities that couples must navigate in an intimate relationship. It is important to remember that, while maintaining a quality relationship comes with its challenges, the benefits far outweigh these costs.

Another common category of relationship problems involves health-related behaviors. This typically involves behavior that affects either a partner's health or the health of the relationship itself. Issues such as alcohol or drug use, poor sleep habits, weight management, and inadequate self-care can all have an impact. When these behaviors become recurrent problems, they can significantly increase stress within the relationship.

In conclusion, a couple's ability to successfully resolve relationship problems is critical for building and maintaining a healthy and stable intimate relationship. Effective problem-solving skills play a key role in protecting a relationship from excessive stress that can weaken its foundation. Learning to resolve issues effectively while managing the emotions that they generate is one of the hallmarks of a strong, resilient long-term relationship.

THE RED ZONE

19

MANAGING RELATIONSHIP STRESS
FROM STRESS TO SUCCESS

Conflicts are inevitable in all relationships. Most of these conflicts will be benign and will not result in any significant harm to a relationship. The most significant factor between success and failure in managing conflicts will be how a couple reacts and manages them.

Relationship problems typically consist of two components: the problem and the emotional reaction to the problem. The focus here will be on emotional reactions and their impact on intimate relationships. The ability to effectively manage emotional stress is a critical difference that separates successful couples from distressed ones. While a couple's ability to resolve problems is often crucial to the success of their relationship, how well they manage their emotions is equally important. Ultimately, the health of an intimate relationship is directly related to how well a couple manages emotions.

Most couples, when addressing problems in the Yellow Zone, understand that these issues can potentially trigger emotional reactions. In these cases, even though emotions may be unpleasant, they are generally managed successfully without causing harm to the relationship. Frequently, emotions require some degree of emotional grit.

In essence, the ability to tolerate and cope with unpleasant emotions should, at times, be expected when addressing problems.

All couples will need to address problems at various points in their relationship, so it is essential that they learn skills to effectively manage emotional responses if they are to achieve a successful, long-term relationship. Fortunately, these skills can be learned, and couples can improve their ability to manage emotional stress in their relationship.

Generally, problems addressed in the Yellow Zone typically cause only mild to moderate emotional reactions, and most couples can manage and navigate their way to the resolution of their problems and the satisfaction of their needs. However, for a significant number of couples, more intense emotional reactions are an issue that causes significant stress on their relationship.

When emotions escalate to a more intense level, many couples lose control over their emotions and say or do things that cause harm to one or both partners. When this occurs, the relationship is now in the phase referred to as the "Red Zone." The Red Zone refers to any situation where one or both partners communicate or behave in ways that are harmful to each other. The Red zone is where most of the significant harm occurs in relationships.

While emotional reactions are present in both the Yellow and Red Zones, the critical difference is how these emotions are expressed and whether they lead to communication or behavior that is harmful or unhealthy to either partner. When this harmful communication or behavior occurs, the health and stability of the relationship will be weakened. This is a significant cost to the relationship that results in the loss of relationship wealth.

The communication and behavior that define the Red Zone often occur after other more reasonable approaches have been tried and failed. Each partner often believes that their own approach was reasonable, and that the other partner was at fault for the emotional escalation. Once either partner feels injured, they believe that they are justified in responding in a similar manner. Once this occurs, one or both partners show little regard for the other and begin to express themselves in mean or hurtful ways.

For many individuals, once emotions escalate, their communication becomes increasingly abrasive, resulting in increased tension, stress, and irritability, which further damages communication. As emotions continue to intensify, the communication often becomes more negative, shifting the couple from the Yellow Zone to the more harmful Red Zone. When this occurs, negative emotions override reason and judgement, leading partners to say or do things that they normally would not. Although most couples recognize the potential harm in this behavior, it is often very difficult to prevent or break the cycle.

Couples who fail to effectively manage harmful, emotionally driven communication and behavior are more likely to spend more time in the Red Zone, increasing the risk of significant damage to their relationship. Therefore, it is critical for couples to develop the ability to regulate emotional reactions to prevent harm and protect the relationship.

Abusive communication and behavior are harmful to both the core and foundation of intimate relationships. It has a ripple effect across the entire relationship and have a significant negative impact on each of the other relationship needs. Under these conditions, it is extremely difficult to maintain a healthy level of security, love, respect, and trust. When one partner is living in an environment of fear and abuse it has the potential to lead to long-term psychological and emotional trauma. Abuse erodes love and intimacy, which makes it extremely difficult to maintain a healthy, supportive relationship. The most frequent outcome is often a broken or failed relationship.

Relationship stress primarily stems from an inability to successfully meet the needs of one or both partners. The frustration that results from unmet needs, combined with a negative or hostile approach to the situation, creates the conditions for intense emotional reactions. The solution to this problem lies in learning to better address each other's needs and adopting a more constructive approach to managing the emotional stress associated with these problems.

Emotional reactions can vary from mild tension and annoyance to intense responses that feel overwhelming and out of control. In most cases, emotions build up gradually, but for many couples, they can flare up suddenly. As emotions intensify, expressing and regulating them becomes much more difficult. Once emotional control is lost, the likelihood of harmful communication and behavior significantly increases.

Emotional reactions to stress can vary greatly among individuals, and the differences between partners can be significant. Some partners may show little to no emotion, while others can be highly expressive. Some individuals may experience strong negative feelings yet remain positive and cooperative when addressing challenging problems. In contrast, other partners might become hostile, critical, or abusive over relatively minor issues.

The intensity of emotional reactions can depend on several factors, including each partner's temperament, the nature of the problem, each partner's interpretation of the problem, and the level of stress that they are experiencing at the time. While intense emotions can be a concern, they are not necessarily harmful to a relationship. Many couples experience strong emotions yet remain happy together. In these cases, partners often accept each other's emotional intensity because their reactions lack negative or harmful elements. In essence, while the emotional intensity may be high, the toxic aspect is absent. Many emotional reactions reflect how important an issue is to one or both partners, rather than an attempt to cause harm to each other.

Of the various emotions involved in problem-solving, anger is by far the most toxic and harmful to relationships. Anger expressed in a mean or hurtful way, even in small amounts, can result in significant harm to a relationship. Anger that is harbored and prolonged is like a cancer to the relationship. One of the primary reasons for this is that the anger it is not only extremely toxic, but it also inhibits the flow of positive feelings.

Angry feelings are experienced by all couples at various points during their relationship. When expressed respectfully, these feelings can have a minimal negative effect. Often, the expression of anger and frustration arises when one or both partners perceive the other as unfair or hurtful. In these cases, appropriately expressing anger or frustration can foster understanding and lead to positive changes within the relationship.

However, when couples communicate or behave in harmful ways toward each other, it negatively affects the flow of positive feelings, such as care and nurturance. As negative emotions increase, positive feelings typically decrease. For instance, when one partner expresses anger or negative behavior, it not only triggers similar behavior in the other partner, but it also reduces motivation, cooperation, and the expression of positive feelings. These negative effects can persist or radiate long after the stressful interaction has ended. Essentially, as harmful communication and behavior increases in the Red Zone, the flow of positive feelings in the Blue Zone reciprocally decreases. In essence, the harmful impact that occurs in the Red Zone reduces and blocks the flow of security, love, nurturance, and pleasure experienced in the Blue Zone.

Red Zone Communication

- Inflammatory language
- An attitude of meanness
- Accusatory
- Derogatory statements
- Critical
- Demanding
- Sarcasm
- Defensiveness
- Not taking responsibility
- No desire to compromise.
- Never or rarely apologizes
- Unsupportive

- Temper reactions
- Extreme emotional reactions
- Minimal tolerance of stress
- Contempt
- Frequent blame and criticism
- Avoidance of issues
- Withdrawal

Patterns of Communication

Couples who frequently experience unmanaged anger and conflict while addressing problems typically fall into one of two major communication patterns. The first is an aggressive pattern, where couples openly express negative communication and behavior. The second is an avoidance pattern, characterized by withdrawal and a reluctance to engage in direct communication about problems. Couples who often find themselves in the Red Zone tend to follow either an aggressive pattern, an avoidance pattern, or a combination of both. These emotionally driven interaction patterns are significant sources of stress in relationships and frequently contribute to the loss of relationship wealth, or even to relationship failure.

Aggressive Pattern

An aggressive pattern of interaction between partners involves any communication or action that causes harm to one or both partners. Hostile or hurtful statements or behaviors such as sarcasm, criticism, insults, ridicule, and threats, can erode the health and stability of a relationship over time.

Such aggressive behavior rarely leads to a mutual resolution of problems. Instead, one partner often feels dominated, while the other grows resentful and angry. This toxic cycle of anger and resentment can linger long after the conflict ends, sometimes lasting hours, days, or even longer.

Aggressive communication patterns are often learned early in life by observing similar behaviors in others. These patterns become reinforced in later relationships and are usually well-established by adulthood. Unfortunately, once ingrained, this approach to problems can persist throughout life, leading to repeated relationship difficulties and a series of failed relationships.

Avoidance Pattern

Another common unhealthy communication pattern in relationships is avoidance. In this case, one or both partners avoid discussing problems and needs, especially when tension or conflict is present. They may either consciously avoid addressing the problem issues or else withdraw from interactions entirely when problems arise.

While aggressive communication is typically driven by anger and frustration, avoidance is usually fueled by anxiety. Those who avoid discussing problems often do so in order to avoid emotional conflict and its potential consequences, such as anger, rejection, criticism, loss of control, or despair. However, this avoidance often leads to anger and frustration in the other partner, who may feel rejected, dismissed, or uncared about.

Like aggressive patterns, avoidance patterns are often learned from early family experiences where parental conflict was either avoided or led to stressful interactions. These experiences create a desire to avoid similar tension and conflict in later relationships.

Partners often have an underlying fear that discussing problems will lead to more conflict or even rejection. They may worry that their partner will leave or that the relationship will fail, especially if there has been a history of arguments involving threats of separation or divorce.

An avoidance pattern may involve steering clear of specific issues or by avoiding any issue that triggers emotional reactions or conflict. This avoidance can take many forms, such as providing only minimal responses, staying silent, claiming to be too busy to talk, changing the subject, or not fully engaging when issues are brought up. Avoidance can also involve dishonesty, such as lying, distorting facts, or omitting important information.

At other times, avoidance can also be an expression of anger. A common example is when one partner gives the other the "silent treatment." While anger is not expressed directly, the underlying emotion behind the silence is often interpreted as anger.

It is important to recognize that both aggressive and avoidance patterns can coexist in a relationship. For example, one partner may be aggressive or hostile, leading the other to become avoidant. This can cause the first partner to become more angry or hostile, or it may lead to their further withdrawal from the conversation.

Couples in distressed relationships often interact with a combination of these patterns when addressing problems. Unfortunately, both aggressive and avoidance behaviors result in unresolved problems, unmet emotional needs, and leave both partners feeling frustrated, angry, and resentful. Whether aggressive or avoidant, these harmful patterns ultimately lead to the same outcome, an unsatisfying relationship with a higher likelihood of failure.

The Cycle of Conflict

For many couples, discussions about problems may begin in a positive and cooperative way, but they can quickly escalate into intense, emotionally charged arguments. Often, couples are unaware of the triggers behind these reactions and continue the conversation without pausing to explore the underlying causes of their emotional responses.

Recognizing emotional triggers is important for managing stress in relationships. An emotional trigger is any communication or behavior that provokes a negative emotional response in one or both partners. Examples include criticism, fault-finding, a hostile tone, frowning, eye-rolling, or other negative words, gestures, or behaviors. In some cases, even the problem being discussed can act an emotional trigger.

During these discussions, each partner listens and thinks about what the other is saying. At any point, something said may be interpreted negatively, triggering an emotional reaction. For example, if one partner criticizes the other, the criticism becomes an emotional trigger. The partner receiving the criticism may interpret it as disrespect, which in turn leads to feelings of anger or hurt. These feelings often cause a defensive or disrespectful reaction, which further escalates the cycle of conflict.

While emotional triggers play a major role in causing stress, it is often the underlying thoughts behind these emotional reactions that drive the emotional escalation. In essence, negative thinking fuels negative emotions, which then lead to negative communication and behavior. This, in turn, provokes an emotional response from the other partner, perpetuating the cycle of conflict.

Breaking this cycle of conflict requires recognizing emotional triggers and understanding the thoughts that drive them. By identifying these triggers, couples can better anticipate when emotional reactions are likely to occur - whether triggered by a specific issue, a word or phrase, or even the tone or attitude of a partner. If emotional triggers are not addressed, the couple is likely to repeat the same destructive patterns throughout their relationship.

Managing Emotional Stress

Successfully managing stress in a relationship requires couples to prevent, neutralize, or de-escalate emotional reactions before they cause harm. The goal is to address relationship problems while preventing emotional responses from disrupting or harming the relationship. The strategies focused on here are effective not only for emotionally challenging conflicts but also in situations where emotions are challenging but still regulated.

Strategies for managing stress in relationships generally fall into two categories. The first involves individual strategies, where each partner takes responsibility for managing their own emotional stress. These methods typically focus on maintaining calm and emotional self-control. Each partner is responsible for monitoring their stress levels and preventing their own emotional escalation. This requires being mindful of one's thoughts, the words chosen, and the attitude that one projects.

The second category includes interaction strategies, which involve actions one partner can take to help the other reduce stress and maintain emotional control. Managing stress is easier and more effective when both partners work together as a team, supporting each other in coping with stress.

A successful approach to managing relationship stress combines both individual and interactive strategies. Using multiple strategies offers the most effective way to reduce stress and leads to the best outcomes for the relationship.

While understanding these strategies is an important first step, the critical next step is the consistent implementation and practice of these skills. Like any ability, managing stress improves with regular practice. Repetition and effort are key to mastering stress management techniques. However, the time and energy invested in stress management provide significant benefits, ultimately enhancing the long-term health and stability of the relationship.

Positive Thought Chain

The first, and perhaps most important, strategy for managing emotional stress is the Positive Thought Chain. This technique involves using a series of positive thoughts to reduce and manage stress. Each thought in the chain contributes to calming emotions and improving self-control. Basically, it is a tool that couples can use to talk themselves down rather than to remain on an inflammatory track.

The goal of the Positive Thought Chain is to consciously replace the negative thoughts that cause emotional distress with ones that neutralize or reduce emotional stress, leading to greater emotional stability. The core of this strategy is intentionally shifting from negative thinking to calming, positive thoughts.

The reason why this strategy works is because emotions follow thinking, whether they are positive or negative. Negative recurrent thoughts tend to intensify emotions, escalating conflicts. By replacing them with a series of positive thoughts, the emotional intensity is reduced, creating a counterbalancing effect that helps reduce tension.

If the negative emotions are justified, it is best to address the issue directly, but only after emotions have calmed and self-control has been regained. Regardless of the situation, the priority should be on managing emotions and maintaining self-control, as it is extremely difficult to resolve any issue effectively under these conditions.

Creating an effective Positive Thought Chain involves writing down a list of thoughts that promote calm and counteract negative thinking. For this strategy to be most effective, each thought must be true, believable, and aligned with the relationship goals one wishes to achieve.

There are many positive or neutralizing thoughts that effectively reduce stress. The examples below can serve as a guide for creating a personalized Positive Thought Chain. It is generally recommended to come up with five to ten calming thoughts that are uniquely meaningful to each partner.

- Everything will be alright.
- I can handle this.
- Calm down first.
- Take a deep breath and slow down.
- What outcome do I want?
- What does my partner need?
- What do I really need right now?
- Should I talk or just listen?
- What can I do or say to calm my partner?
- Frustration and stress are normal – I can handle it.
- I can listen with compassion.
- I will focus on understanding the issue, not the frustration.
- Why is this issue so important to my partner?

- We both want a solution.
- The health of my relationship matters more than this issue.
- I can take a break and come back to this later if needed.
- What is there really to worry about?
- I want to give my partner space to express their feelings.

The Positive Thought Chain becomes increasingly effective with repeated use. Initially, when one or both partners are emotionally overwhelmed, it can feel difficult to shift to positive thinking. For this reason, it is important to stay deliberately focused on positive and neutralizing thoughts long enough for them to take effect and calm the situation.

Relaxation Response

A second tool for managing emotional stress is using Progressive Muscle Relaxation and deep breathing techniques. When under stress, the body naturally become tense, initiating a fight/ flight reaction. This reaction creates a high level of energy that can be difficult to regulate because it is geared toward physical action. Progressive muscle relaxation helps to counterbalance this state by directing this energy into a positive direction. This can be achieved through deep breathing exercises combined with progressive muscle relaxation techniques.

The combination of deep breathing, progressive muscle relaxation, and mindfulness have all been shown to reduce stress (Lindsey, 2019). Each of these techniques requires practice to become effective in managing stress.

Calming Imagery

A third self-calming strategy is to visualize calming images, using guided imagery to create a sense of calm. This technique involves imagining a place that has a soothing effect, such as a favorite vacation spot, a serene beach, mountains, or a peaceful forest.

When applied to stress management in relationships, it can be particularly helpful to picture oneself successfully navigating a challenging conflict with a partner. For instance, visualizing a recurring relationship issue, but instead of focusing on the problem, imagining a successful resolution. Picture listening compassionately and offering support, leading to a positive outcome. This success imagery can help to prepare for handling future situations more effectively.

During periods of intense emotional stress, one effective technique is to visualize a raging river that symbolizes one's emotions. Imagine standing at a safe distance, calmly observing the rushing water as you take deep breaths, picturing the river gradually slowing down, allowing tension to release along with it.

These visualization techniques can be powerful tools for coping with emotional stress and, with consistent practice, they become second nature. Combining success imagery, deep breathing, progressive muscle relaxation, and the Positive Thought Chain offers an effective set of strategies for effectively managing stress.

Compassionate Listening

Managing stress in a relationship involves both emotional self-regulation and strategies that focus on the partner. One key partner-focused strategy for reducing stress is compassionate listening. As previously mentioned, listening helps reveal the underlying needs driving emotional reactions.

Compassionate listening is a powerful way to show caring that significantly reduces a partner's emotional stress. When one partner listens with empathy, the other not only feels understood but also feels relieved, since expressing their thoughts and feelings helps to reduce tension. In contrast, poor listening or frequent interruptions tend to increase tension and stress.

Sustaining compassionate listening can be challenging, especially when one or both partners are feeling frustrated or angry. However, developing and maintaining this skill is extremely helpful for managing stress successfully. Listening fosters a deeper understanding, which increases the ability to find solutions that further reduces stress. Additionally, it promotes harmonious communication and encourages a cooperative, team-oriented mindset.

Supportive Communication

Just as with listening, stress can also be reduced when one partner offers support through words and actions. Encouraging a partner to express their feelings, asking a partner questions for clarity, or acknowledging a partner's viewpoint can all to help ease emotional tension.

Additionally, certain communication techniques, such as slowing the pace of speech, reducing the volume, and using a softer, more calming tone, can further reduce emotional intensity and help relieve stress.

Maintaining self-control during periods of high stress often encourages a partner to respond similarly. It's important to remember that, just as anger can be contagious, so too can calmness and compassion. Essentially, the positive or negative communication from one partner tends to influence the other in a similar way. Therefore, engaging in a stressful conversation while effectively managing negative emotions contributes significantly to reducing harmful stress.

The strategies outlined here are helpful in any situation in which emotions run high. The goal of stress management is to prevent, reduce, and resolve harmful emotional reactions that could negatively impact the long-term health and stability of the relationship. By practicing these strategies, couples are better equipped to manage emotional stress and protect the health, wealth, and stability of their relationship.

There are multiple other resources that offer strategies and techniques for managing emotions and preventing the escalation of stress. Greenberg (2017) offers suggestions on using mindfulness, cognitive reframing, self-compassion, and other emotional regulation techniques. Lindsey (2019) provides practical hands-on tools for reducing stress, including the use of mood tracking, self-awareness exercises, and building a "Stress Profile."

A motivated couple can develop the ability to manage stress effectively by practicing a variety of proven strategies and techniques. With consistent effort, partners can strengthen their ability to regulate emotions, reduce stress triggers, and communicate more constructively. Still, there will be times when one or both partners become overwhelmed, and the conflict escalates into the Red Zone. In such moments, a different approach becomes necessary to de-escalate the situation so that harmful communication does not cause harm to the relationship.

Disengagement

When emotional reactions escalate to the point where aggressive language or behavior occurs and self-control is lost, the relationship becomes vulnerable. At this stage, the likelihood of a positive outcome is very low, while the risk of harm to the relationship increases significantly. It is crucial for couples to take immediate steps to prevent further harm.

In such moments, disengaging from the issue becomes the only rational choice. The goal shifts to de-escalating the situation and restoring emotional stability. While emotional reactions can occur suddenly, emotional de-escalation is a slower process that can take time, often lingering for a while. During this period, the risk of additional emotional flare-ups remains high. Couples must remind themselves that the issue can be addressed and resolved later when tensions have eased.

During these situations, disengaging from the issue is the only rational choice. The focus shifts to de-escalation, which helps prevent further escalation and protects the relationship from harm. The primary goal is to protect the relationship. The stressful issue can be addressed later, when emotions have settled down and self-control has been restored.

For the disengagement strategy to be most effective, both partners need to agree in advance to use it when necessary. It is important that they do not see disengagement as a negative response or as an attempt to avoid the issue, but rather as an act of care and as a commitment to protecting the relationship. This approach is about managing emotional reactions wisely to prevent all of the damage that emotional escalation can cause when left unchecked.

Disengagement is an essential tool for managing emotional reactions before they cause harm. However, disengaging from a heated discussion or argument can be extremely difficult, as intense emotions increase the urge to remain engaged. The decision to disengage occurs at a critical point in the stress management process and requires cooperation from both partners to be effective.

Disengagement means taking a temporary break from the stressful issue, not from one's partner. Although difficult in such situations, it is important to remain emotionally engaged to prevent one's partner from feeling rejected or dismissed.

In cases where aggressive communication or behavior persists or escalates, it may be necessary for partners to not only disengage from the discussion but also from each other. This can be done by shifting to another activity or going for a walk to cool off. As partners improve their skill in disengagement, the need for physical separation decreases.

It is important to distinguish between disengaging from a problem and avoiding it. Disengagement is a temporary break taken to manage stress and protect the relationship, with the understanding that the issue will be addressed later, when both partners are in a better emotional state.

While disengagement is an essential part of stress management, re-engagement is equally important. Relationship issues are resolved when couples engage with each other and work together to address them. However, this requires both partners to adopt a cooperative, team-oriented approach to managing relationship problems and stress.

A Team Approach

Couples in successful relationships adopt a unified, team-oriented approach when dealing with relationship problems and emotional stress. They understand the importance of preventing and managing emotional reactions during conflict. In emotionally tense discussions, they not only protect each other but also safeguard their relationship. This protective mindset helps them to regulate their emotions more effectively and maintain self-control.

Successful couples approach their problems strategically and, as a result, rarely experience intense emotional reactions. A key reason for this is their ability to meet each other's needs in a satisfying way. This reduces the frustration and dissatisfaction that can trigger unhealthy emotional reactions. Additionally, successful couples share mutual respect and a strong commitment to resolving conflicts cooperatively, both of which help to sustain a healthy, long-term relationship.

The simplest and most effective way that successful couples prevent and minimize emotional stress is by establishing a structured team agreement, which clearly defines the rules of engagement when addressing emotionally stressful problems. This agreement serves as the foundation for effectively managing relationship stress by outlining how, when, and where issues will be addressed. It also provides clarity as to what is and is not acceptable when expressing stress related emotions.

In conclusion, problems and emotional stress are a normal part of every relationship. The more difficult a problem is, the greater the potential for emotional reactions to escalate, leading to harmful communication and behavior that can damage the relationship's health and quality. The success or failure of an intimate relationship often depends on how well couples manage their emotions, which enables their relationship to remain stable and healthy over time.

Managing relationship stress is an essential need in any intimate relationship. Couples who invest in developing the skills necessary to manage relationship stress become better equipped to handle the inevitable stresses that occur when addressing relationship issues and conflicts. These skills, essentially, protect the relationship from the stress that occurs when addressing relationship issues and problems. By doing so, couples can build and preserve relationship wealth, allowing them to enjoy a more satisfying and lasting relationship.

RELATIONSHIP WEALTH IN ACTION

20

INVESTING IN THE FUTURE

The central theme of this book is that great meaning and satisfaction in life comes from successful intimate relationships. This perspective suggests that, among the various forms of wealth, relationship wealth may be the most meaningful and deeply desired. It is, in essence, the cement that forms the foundation of all successful relationships.

Relationship wealth is not based on luck or mere good fortune, nor does it come freely. Instead, it is earned through consistent investments of time, effort, and love. Anyone willing to commit themselves to this goal has the potential to cultivate a long-lasting, loving relationship. With deliberate and sustained practice, a deeply satisfying and fulfilling intimate relationship can be achieved.

Research has shown that there are many diverse pathways to achieve a successful relationship, each one having its own unique experience. However, all successful relationships share a common foundation of core relationship needs that determine its strength and health.

By understanding and meeting the core relationship needs, each individual and couple can establish a roadmap to build and maintain a healthy, enduring relationship. Through dedication and commitment to meeting these needs, couples can build relationship wealth and achieve a fulfilling, lifelong relationship.

Relationship wealth, in essence, consists of the positive emotions, thoughts, and experiences that create and support the perceived value of a relationship. This value is reinforced by the consistent satisfaction of sixteen essential needs that serve as the foundation of the relationship. As previously described, these essential relationship needs fall into four categories or zones – Blue, Green, Yellow, and Red. Each of these zones, and the needs within them, play a major role in the well-being and health of a relationship. Couples in healthy relationships flow in and out of these zones, depending on the current needs of the relationship. When these needs are satisfied, couples experience a positive relationship flow, and they transition smoothly between each of the zones, thereby enhancing the stability of the relationship.

Couples in successful relationships understand these needs and have the expectation that investing in their relationship is an ongoing lifelong process. They invest their time, energy, and heart into meeting each other's needs for love, nurturance, pleasure, and security. Emphasis is primarily placed on the needs of the Blue Zone, because this is where a significant part of relationship wealth is derived. Successful couples understand that the neglect of these needs causes stress to accumulate within the relationship, which leads to a loss of relationship wealth.

Successful couples also focus on fine tuning their communication, continuously striving to better understand each other's thinking, feelings, and needs. Much of the work in building successful relationships occurs during periods when couples connect with each other. These points of connection are, in essence, the basic element or building block of a relationship. It is where all communication occurs, love is expressed, time is shared, and the life of the relationship exists. Each of these points of connection presents an opportunity to improve and strengthen the relationship. Every word and action have the potential to contribute to building relationship wealth and strengthening the emotional bond between partners.

In the Green Zone, successful couples function together as a team, based on trust, respect, honesty, loyalty, leadership, commitment, fairness, and friendship. These needs form the backbone of a strong and stable relationship. Most couples spend most of their time in the Green Zone, focused on managing and meeting day-to-day needs. The stability in this zone is directly related to how well the needs in other zones are met.

Building and maintaining a successful relationship requires that couples effectively manage the challenges and problems that inevitably occur in all relationships. In the Yellow Zone, it is necessary to have effective tools and strategies to maintain the stability and success of the relationship. It is here that problems are defined, solutions are explored, and agreements are reached. However, it is also a time and place where emotional stress can be significant. To avoid instability and stress on the relationship, it is essential to manage emotions while addressing problems in this zone. The ability to successfully resolve problems and conflicts will have a direct impact on the overall quality and health of the relationship. The most effective couples are those who adopt a team-oriented approach to the prevention and management of stress in their relationship while in this zone.

In the Red Zone, problems can often create significant negative emotional reactions. Therefore, it is important to maintain an ongoing awareness that communication and behavior can easily become harmful in this zone. To maintain a successful relationship, couples should adhere to guidelines that protect their relationship from the toxic effects of the Red Zone. Successful couples generally avoid ending up in this zone by agreeing to disengage well before emotions escalate to a harmful level.

In general, relationships do not have to be perfect to be successful. There are times in any relationship when one or both partners can become discouraged or disheartened with the relationship or with their partner. Positive emotions and moods can ebb and flow. During these times it is helpful to return to the principles previously outlined and reset the leadership plan by redefining the goals and needs of the relationship. During difficult times, the power of one's communication through thoughtful words, meaningful actions, and genuine expressions of love are often enough to overcome any challenge.

The future stability and health of one's relationship hinges not just on what is done today, but on the investments of time, love, and care expressed over the long term. The motivation and desire to maintain this commitment is what ultimately achieves the greatest relationship wealth. Although challenging to sustain, the principles outlined in this book, when practiced consistently and intentionally, can significantly improve the stability and quality of almost any relationship. Every day presents an opportunity to invest in the relationship, and every interaction provides a chance to strengthen the connection and deepen the emotional bond between partners.

For many couples there is a tendency to become complacent and take their relationship for granted. Over time, it is easy to become desensitized and less appreciative of the significant value that a quality relationship holds. It is essential to guard against this tendency, as it can easily and stealthily erode the quality of the relationship. Rather than build relationship wealth, complacency and taking one's partner for granted can diminish relationship wealth over time. An effective way to prevent relationship complacency is to periodically take the time necessary to discuss and explore new ways to stimulate the relationship. Just having such a conversation can serve to demonstrate care, value, and appreciation of each partner for the other, and restore value to the relationship.

Having a satisfying and fulfilling relationship is a precious gift that brings great fortune to those who have it. Many people long for such a connection but have not been able to find or sustain one. Being in a great relationship is a profound treasure that should be appreciated and cherished. However, it can also be fragile and can be lost without proper care. As with anything in life that holds great value, a quality relationship requires love, effort, and support to build and sustain.

For many, creating and nurturing a loving relationship is one of life's most valuable investments, and one which offers profound meaning and purpose. Love is a conscious choice and a priceless opportunity to dedicate one's heart to a shared lifelong journey. There is no greater wealth than that of the pleasure and emotional richness found in a deep, loving relationship. This book provides a blueprint for creating and sustaining a successful, lifelong relationship, full of happiness, love, and the relationship wealth to last a lifetime.

APPENDIX A - RELATIONSHIP ZONES

THE RELATIONSHIP ZONES

BLUE ZONE

Love

- Affection
- Intimacy
- Attraction factors
- Channels of caring
- Passion

Nurturance

- Caring
- Encouragement
- Emotional support
- Compassion
- Compliments

Pleasure

- Fun activities
- Sense of humor
- Playfulness
- Shared enjoyment
- Happiness

Security

- Safety / Security
- Stability
- Reassurance
- Financial security

GREEN ZONE

- Communication
- Trust
- Respect
- Honesty
- Loyalty
- Teamwork
- Leadership
- Commitment
- Fairness
- Friendship

YELLOW ZONE

- Problem Management

RED ZONE

- Stress Management

APPENDIX B - RELATIONSHIP WEALTH SCALE

Rate the level of satisfaction in your relationship with each quality below on a scale from 0 to 5.

    0 – None

    1 – Very little

    2 - Marginal

    3 - Moderate

    4 - High

    5 – Very high

Overall level of satisfaction with your relationship:

    Trust

    Caring

    Sense of humor

    Ability to listen

    Honesty

    Empathy

    Respect

    Talkative

    Fairness

    Tolerance

Common interests

Problem - solving

Loyalty

Playfulness

Attitude

Protective

Generosity

Openness

Acceptance

Time spent together

Communication

Expression of feelings

Managing Stress

Appreciation

Commitment

Ability to forgive

Love

Teamwork

Security

Ability to compromise

Financial security

Feeling loved

Contentment

Sharing

Pleasure

Passion

Emotional support

Happiness

Affection / intimacy

Dependability

Emotional control

Safety

Friendship

Independence

Leadership

Encouragement
Understanding needs
Patience
Compassion
Independence

Total Score:

Level of Relationship Wealth
    High: 150 – 250
    Moderate: 100 – 150
    Marginal: 50 – 100
    Distressed: Below 50

APPENDIX C - RELATIONSHIP AGREEMENTS

RELATIONSHIP AGREEMENTS

All successful couples depend on a number of relationship agreements. These agreements serve the purpose of helping a relationship to run more smoothly and efficiently, resulting in less conflict and emotional distress, which can have a significant negative impact on the health and quality of a relationship.

The following relationship agreements are basic agreements that can be used to help better structure and define what each partner desires and needs in their relationship. This serves the needs of both partners, increases relationship wealth, and reduces stress on the relationship. Each of the agreements outlined can be modified to meet the specific and unique needs of each couple. Periodically reviewing these agreements is suggested since needs and circumstances change over time in most relationships.

Type of Agreement

Relationship Trust Agreement

Communication Agreement

Commitment Agreement

Loyalty Agreement

Respect Agreement

Leadership Agreement

Team Agreement

Honesty Agreement

Fairness Agreement

Intimacy and Nurturance Agreement

Security Agreement

Problem-solving Agreement

Stress Management Agreement

RELATIONSHIP TRUST AGREEMENT

We recognize and mutually agree that trust is an essential pillar of our relationship. To nurture and maintain trust in our relationship, we agree to uphold the following principles to support trust and emotional security:

1. Building Trust

- Acknowledge that trust forms the essential foundation of all healthy relationships.
- Consistently strive to build and maintain absolute trust in each other.
- Make decisions that reflect dependability and reliability.
- Maintain commitment and loyalty.
- Always act in the best interests of the relationship.
- Encourage individual and shared goals to deepen connection and trust.

2. Security

- Create an environment free from physical, emotional, or psychological harm.
- Avoid any form of verbal or physical threats, abuse, or intimidation.
- Identify and consistently promote each other's needs for security and emotional safety.

3. Honesty

- Maintain complete honesty and openness in communication.
- Discuss issues, feelings, and concerns openly and honestly, no matter how difficult.
- Practice integrity in what you do and how you do it.

4. Self-Disclosure

- Openly share thoughts, emotions, and experiences with transparency.
- Encourage open expression and support one another's areas of vulnerability.
- Create a safe environment for being authentic and emotionally available to each other.

5. Dependability

- Strive to be consistently reliable and dependable in all commitments.
- Follow through on promises and agreements made with each other.
- Maintain consistency in words and actions.
- Be reliable and accountable for living up to all relationship agreements.

6. Commitment

- Commit to dedicating effort and attention to building and maintaining trust.
- Recognize that trust is dynamic and must be continually nurtured.
- Respect each other's needs for autonomy, privacy, and personal space.

7. Trust in Physical and Emotional Intimacy

- Define needs and desires for physical and emotional intimacy.
- Respect each other's boundaries regarding physical and emotional intimacy.

- Create time to express preferences, hesitations, or concerns without fear or shame.

8. Finances

- Value transparency and open dialogue about financial matters.
- Share financial obligations, expectations, and decisions responsibly.
- Promote trust by disclosing all aspects of finances that impact the relationship.

9. Privacy and Confidentiality

- Respect and protect each other's personal privacy.
- Avoid sharing sensitive or personal relationship information with others.
- Maintain healthy personal boundaries necessary for sustaining mutual trust.

10. Risks to Trust

- Prevent and avoid communication and behaviors that undermine trust.
- Do not omit information that would be needed to have a clear understanding of an issue.
- Avoid making decisions unilaterally that should be made as a team to prevent the erosion of trust.
- Avoid manipulative or passive-aggressive communication.
- Speak truthfully in a supportive manner during conflict, disagreement, and distress.
- Protect the relationship from statements, actions, or social interactions that may harm or compromise trust, directly or indirectly.

- Avoid secrecy or ambiguity in interactions with others that may be misinterpreted or compromise trust and emotional security.
- Demonstrate consistency between words and actions - say what you mean and mean what you say.

11. Early Intervention in Trust Issues

- Address trust-related concerns in a timely manner when they arise.
- Approach trust issues with sensitivity and support to preserve trust and dignity.
- When feelings of jealousy or anxiety arise related to trust, agree to discuss the issue openly and with compassion.
- Express negative feelings constructively and without accusation, negativity, or hostility.
- After tension or conflict, make a conscious effort to emotionally reconnect.
- Treat moments of repair as opportunities to deepen intimacy and rebuild trust.

12. Repairing Trust

- When trust is violated in some way, we agree that it will be addressed as an immediate priority and will not avoid talking about the issue.
- Agree to immediately discontinue the communication or behavior that caused the breach.
- Avoid blame, accusations, defensiveness, avoidance, and negativity during this process.
- Clearly express an attitude that reflects genuine care, support, and compassion.
- Develop a clear plan of how and when to discuss trust issues to understand the cause of the mistrust and insecurity.

- Identify recovery needs so that the stability of our relationship can be established.
- Develop a revised trust agreement to address any issue or need that may have contributed to the trust problem.
- During the process of revising the trust agreement offer genuine reassurance to prevent unnecessary feelings insecurity.
- Take full responsibility for any breach of trust without excuses or blame.
- Express genuine remorse and empathy regarding the emotional pain and distress that the trust issue has caused.
- Offer a genuine heart-felt apology and a desire to restore trust in the relationship.
- Provide forgiveness to work toward healing and restoring trust.
- Seek professional guidance to help resolve any ongoing issues or stress that has not been adequately resolved.

Through these commitments, we pledge to make every effort to support the need for trust in our relationship. We mutually agree to maintain a genuine effort to build and support unconditional trust in our relationship.

COMMUNICATION AGREEMENT

We recognize that effective communication is one of the most important needs in intimate relationships. The strength, quality, and durability of our relationship depends on how well we speak, listen, and understand each other. To support this essential need, we commit to the following principles:

1. Understanding the Need for Communication

- Acknowledge that communication is essential for meeting relationship needs and to maintain a healthy, long-term relationship.
- Commit to improving communication as a tool to meet needs, increase emotional connection, solve problems and conflicts, and to improve overall relationship quality.
- View communication not just as a series of words or ideas but as an act of love.

2. General Guidelines

- Create a positive tone and mindset before speaking.
- Begin all communication on a positive note, especially when addressing stressful issues.
- Define and set times that will be conducive to good communication, particularly when addressing challenging or emotionally charged topics.
- Avoid bringing up highly sensitive issues during high-stress periods, where possible.
- Encourage the full expression of each partner's point of view.
- Respond to all expressions of communication respectfully.
- Strive to end all conversations on a neutral or positive note.

- Be mindful that some aspect of communication could be misunderstood.

3. Verbal Communication

- Express needs, feelings, and ideas clearly and respectfully.
- Use a warm, calm, and attentive tone when speaking.
- Use positive words and gestures to reinforce mutual affection and respect.
- Speak respectfully, particularly during conflict.
- Use encouraging, affirming, and appreciative language.
- Follow the 5-question rule - Ask 5 or more questions until there is mutual agreement that a clear understanding has been reached.
- Focus on one issue or topic at a time.
- Communicate using "we" rather than "I" to reinforce the team perspective.
- Begin conversations with positive statements.
- State needs directly and constructively.
- Recognize and comment on positive statements made.
- If emotions increase, slow down the pace of speaking.
- Encourage partner to openly express their thoughts, emotions, and concerns.
- Seek feedback to confirm mutual understanding.
- When misunderstood – clarify what was meant in order to correct misunderstandings.
- Ask for feedback to confirm shared understanding.

4. Listening

- Commit to listening with focus, patience, and presence.
- Use active listening to understand first, to prevent drawing faulty conclusions.
- Practice intentional listening to build understanding, emotional closeness, and trust.

- Prioritize listening and understanding over responding.
- Listen for points of agreement first before addressing differences.
- Use empathy to understand your partner's experience and perspective.
- Use the SEND method, where S represents the subject being discussed, E for the emotion experienced, N for the primary need, and D for what to do in response.
- Listen without interrupting or judging.
- Respond in ways that show understanding and empathy.

5. Nonverbal Communication

- Pay attention to nonverbal cues – tone of voice, facial expressions, etc.
- Be mindful of your own tone and facial expression when listening or speaking.
- Use positive nonverbal communication - smile, eye contact, and supportive touch.
- Maintain eye contact and acknowledge what is being said through nodding.
- Manage internal emotions to prevent the escalation of stress.

6. Avoiding Common Problems in Communication

- Assume that there may be misunderstandings.
- Avoid destructive communication patterns that involve criticism, sarcasm, shaming, or verbal abuse.
- Avoid negative nonverbal cues such as a hostile tone, eye-rolling, or finger-pointing.
- Be aware of emotional reactions that can escalate the stress level.
- Avoid focusing on what you plan to say instead of listening to your partner.

- Avoid silence or withdrawal as a replacement for meaningful, respectful engagement.
- Rather than automatically giving advice, ask if they would be open to a suggestion.
- Avoid reacting defensively or in a hostile tone.

7. Reconnection after Conflict

- Prioritize reconnection over being right.
- Re-engage in a positive way, conveying a desire to reconnect.
- Acknowledge the fact that each partner's emotions are real and valid, even though there may not be agreement on a particular issue or point of view.
- Focus on solutions instead of blame.
- Take responsibility and apologize for one's role in the conflict or misunderstanding.
- Acknowledge that, in the end, it's not who is right but what is right for the relationship.

We agree to prioritize and continuously improve our communication as a core component of our relationship's strength and success. Through effective speaking and intentional listening, we commit to building a foundation of clarity, empathy, trust, and lasting emotional connection.

RELATIONSHIP COMMITMENT AGREEMENT

We, as partners, acknowledge and affirm the essential importance of our commitment to each other and to our relationship. Recognizing that genuine commitment contributes to trust, emotional security, and relationship stability, we mutually agree to uphold the following principles:

1. Mutual Devotion

- Commit fully to each other's well-being and the health of the relationship.
- Dedicate ourselves to meeting the needs of the relationship.
- Commit the time and effort necessary to build and maintain a long-term healthy relationship.

2. A Shared Vision and Meaning

- Remind ourselves of the emotional and rational reasons for our commitment, such as sharing love, connection, and physical and emotional needs.
- Build a shared purpose or vision of our future together.
- Support those activities that strengthen and preserve commitment.

3. Open Communication

- Ensure that communication is supportive, respectful, and constructive.
- Be responsive to individual and shared needs in the relationship.
- Express commitment regularly through words and actions.
- Talk about future goals, plans, and dreams.

4. Trust and Reliability

- Consistently support each other's needs, especially during stress.
- Make every effort not to undermine trustworthiness in any aspect of our relationship.
- Ensure and reinforce the belief that we can depend on each other.

5. Aligned Values and Compatibility

- Recognize that compatibility is vital to our commitment.
- Discuss significant differences openly and respectfully.
- Establish harmony in family values, finances, lifestyle, and intimacy.
- Show that your partner matters to you.

6. Commitment Through Shared Goals

- Define and plan shared relationship goals.
- Align decisions with our long-term vision for our relationship and for our life together.
- Periodically review and renew the importance of our commitment.
- Openly discuss changing needs, feelings, and concerns.
- Address issues that may weaken commitment.

7. Facing Insecurities with Courage

- Face relationship challenges with compassion and openness.
- Address underlying fears and vulnerabilities associated with commitment.
- Work constructively to prevent issues from undermining our commitment.

- Prioritize emotional safety and growth for both partners.
- Avoid words or actions that undermine commitment.

8. Commitment Choice

- Reinforce a complete and unconditional commitment to each other, even during periods of stress.
- Address any issue that may undermine commitment or the stability of the relationship.
- Make a commitment to meet our needs for emotional security, love, and trust.
- Avoid implying that commitment is conditional during periods of stress.

9. Investment and Sacrifice

- Acknowledge and accept that commitment involves time, energy, and personal sacrifice.
- Consistently invest the time needed to nurture the health of our relationship.
- Make intentional time for each other.
- Recognize that the benefits of our commitment outweigh the challenges.
- Reaffirm commitment over time to reinforce the desire to maintain commitment.

Through adherence to these principles, we commit ourselves to building and sustaining a healthy, stable, and emotionally fulfilling lifelong partnership. This agreement will allow us to maintain a healthy and satisfying commitment to our relationship that can endure everyday problems and challenges.

RELATIONSHIP LOYALTY AGREEMENT

We, as partners, mutually acknowledge and agree that loyalty serves as a critical part of our relationship. We recognize loyalty as being essential for long-term stability, emotional security, and trust within our partnership. With that shared understanding, we commit to the following principles:

1. Mutual Commitment to Loyalty

- Maintain a committed, exclusive relationship built on mutual trust.
- Honor fidelity in all aspects of our relationship.
- Prioritize each other's well-being, emotional needs, and security.

2. Physical Fidelity

- Commit to complete sexual exclusivity.
- Define and honor clearly defined boundaries around physical intimacy.
- Avoid physical or affectionate behaviors that compromise trust or intimacy.

3. Emotional Loyalty

- Maintain healthy emotional boundaries with those outside of the relationship.
- Avoid actions that suggest romantic or inappropriate emotional intimacy with others.
- Stay emotionally connected to each other as the primary source of romantic support.

4. Social Loyalty

- Strive for balance between personal connections and our shared partnership.
- Support each other's friendships while prioritizing emotional commitment.
- Ensure that outside relationships do not interfere with commitment to loyalty.
- Uphold mutual respect in all social settings, whether together or apart.
- Defend each other against criticism, negativity, or harmful comments.
- Avoid sharing private information that could damage trust.

5. Financial Loyalty

- Practice complete openness and honesty in all financial matters.
- Disclose debts, expenses, assets, and financial decisions that could affect our relationship.
- Avoid financial secrecy and behaviors that may harm our financial health or trust.

6. Spiritual Loyalty

- Respect and support each other's spiritual or religious beliefs and practices.
- Communicate openly about spiritual needs and expectations.
- Uphold mutual respect for spiritual differences to support relationship harmony.

7. Communication, Boundaries, and Trust

- Define what loyalty means in our relationship.

- Discuss and clarify expectations, boundaries, and concerns.
- Share insecurities and fears to build mutual trust and emotional closeness.
- Communicate honestly about situations that could lead to conflict, distance, or misunderstanding.
- Recognize that divided attention can feel like emotional absence over time.

8. Loyalty in Conflict

- Avoid betraying each other during moments of conflict by name-calling, public shaming, or threats to the relationship.
- Maintain respect and a sense of commitment even when emotions are heightened.
- Never use personal vulnerabilities as weapons during disagreements.
- Approach stressful situations with empathy and supportive communication.
- Reaffirm loyalty, even in disagreement, to protect the emotional integrity of the relationship.

9. Prevention, Awareness, and Emotional Protection

- Be aware of potential risks to loyalty and address them early.
- Take responsibility for protecting the relationship from situations that could cause harm.
- Focus on preventing emotional damage and maintaining relational integrity.
- Recognize the harm disloyalty causes and commit to safeguarding each other's emotional wellbeing.

10. Loyalty in Absence

- Support emotional and physical commitment during times of physical separation.
- Maintain physical and emotional boundaries of loyalty while apart.
- Speak respectfully about your partner in their absence.

ii. Loyalty Through Life Transitions

- Stay emotionally and practically devoted through major life changes.
- Offer increased care and presence when one partner needs extra support.
- Maintain a sense of "we" while honoring individual identity.
- Align personal actions with shared values and commitments to guide actions through all seasons of life.

Through adherence to these principles, we commit ourselves to sustaining loyalty throughout our life together. This agreement outlines our needs for loyalty to each other and to our relationship, necessary to sustain a healthy and satisfying long-term relationship.

RESPECT AGREEMENT

We, as partners, mutually agree to uphold respect as part of the foundation within our relationship, and recognize its significance in maintaining the health, stability, and quality of our partnership. Accordingly, we commit to the following principals:

1. Mutual Respect

- Consistently treat each other with a positive and respectful attitude.
- Show regard for each other's dignity, feelings, and well-being.
- Offer recognition, attention, and thoughtfulness in both behavior and communication.
- Reinforce mutual value and care through respectful actions and words.
- Follow through on promises, agreements, and commitments as a show of respect.
- Be reliable and dependable in both words and actions.
- When mistakes are made, apologize and take responsibility for words or actions.

2. Self-Respect

- Take responsibility for one's physical, emotional, and social needs.
- Recognize the need for self-care.
- Encourage each other to maintain self-respect.

3. Acceptance

- Accept each other, including strengths, flaws, differences, and unique traits.

- Refrain from judgment, unnecessary criticism, or efforts to control.
- Create a safe environment that encourages personal expression and authenticity.
- Support each other's personal growth, including changes in goals, beliefs, or habits.
- Accept that change is a natural part of long-term relationships.

4. Respectful Communication

- Maintain respectful communication, particularly during times of disagreement or conflict.
- Practice active listening, without interruption.
- Allow each other to fully express thoughts, emotions, and opinions.
- Respond with thoughtfulness, compassion, and patience.
- Avoid criticism, negative judgment, and disrespectful language or tone.
- Encourage independent thought and self-expression in all decisions.
- Offer suggestions without pressure or control with regards to making personal choices.
- Practice shared decision-making, particularly those decisions that affect both partners.

5. Independence and Personal Growth

- Respect each other's need for independence, privacy, and personal space.
- Support the pursuit of individual passions and self-growth.
- Encourage and honor friendships and meaningful connections outside the relationship.

- Actively support and encourage each other's goals, dreams, and personal interests.
- Promote both individual and shared growth with encouragement and support.

6. Respect for Relationship Needs

- Prioritize the emotional, relationship, and practical needs of the partnership.
- Invest in communication and behaviors that nurture relationship health.
- Readily make sacrifices or compromises for the benefit of the relationship's wellbeing.
- Acknowledge and honor each other's time, schedules, and energy levels.
- Show appreciation for everyday contributions (e.g., work, caregiving, emotional labor).

7. Social Respect

- Respect and nurture both shared and individual social relationships.
- Recognize the importance of a healthy social network for emotional balance and support.
- Encourage one another to maintain fulfilling connections that support individual needs.
- Maintain the positive image of one's partner, whether together or not.

8. Respect in Conflict Resolution

- Avoid disrespectful communication and behaviors during conflict, such as sarcasm, name-calling, stonewalling, or raising your voice.
- Regulate and manage emotions during periods of stress.

- Commit to de-escalation and repair rather than "winning" the argument.
- Respect each other's emotional limits and provide space when needed.
- Avoid withdrawal and isolation when emotionally distressed.
- Allow each other time to express and process emotions.
- Avoid rushing or dismissing your partner's emotional experience.

By mutually honoring the principals of this agreement, we will be better able to support the health and dignity of our relationship. Through our mutual respect we will honor our relationship and work toward building a healthy and durable relationship.

RELATIONSHIP LEADERSHIP AGREEMENT

We, as partners, mutually agree that leadership plays a major role in our ability to meet the needs of our relationship. We agree and commit to a model of leadership that supports both independence and healthy interdependence so that our relationship can achieve the highest level of stability, quality, and emotional satisfaction. For these reasons, we commit ourselves to the following principles:

1. Mutual Commitment to Leadership

- Acknowledge the importance of effective leadership for a healthy, long-term relationship.
- Build and maintain relationship wealth by mutual effort.
- Create opportunities for relationship growth, satisfaction, and stability.
- Celebrate achievements and milestones to reinforce commitment.
- Continuously express gratitude to strengthen bonds.

2. Self-Leadership

- Take responsibility for one's own emotional and practical needs.
- Develop personal care plans, avoiding over-reliance on one's partner.
- Communicate personal needs to maintain balance and respect.
- Reflect regularly on personal growth and areas for improvement.
- Take responsibility for mistakes with humility.
- Cultivate resilience and the ability to adapt to challenging or stressful situations.

3. Co-Leadership

- Share leadership responsibilities in a fair and equitable way.
- Encourage each other's unique strengths and contributions.
- Ensure inclusive and respectful decision-making.
- Explore each other's views, perspectives, and vision.
- Avoid dominating the leadership role.
- Respect and encourage the expression of each other's strengths.
- Encourage teamwork and a joint effort in meeting relationship needs.

4. Communication and Leadership

- Maintain open, respectful communication.
- Ensure each partner has a meaningful voice.
- Collaborate through honest dialogue.
- Avoid negative criticism, judgement, or sarcasm.
- Encourage emotional availability and thoughtful expression.
- Practice active listening in order to understand each other's viewpoints.
- Regularly "check-in" to maintain clear communication.

5. A Shared Vision

- Clearly define mutual goals and long-term aspirations.
- Use shared vision as guidance for relationship decisions.
- Periodically revisit the team vision to maintain a cohesive perspective.
- Align individual goals with relationship goals.

6. Relationship Plan

- Develop a detailed plan for individual and mutual needs.
- Regularly review and adjust the plan.
- Build flexibility and adaptability into the plan.
- Model desired relationship values and ethics.
- Explore ways to create meaningful experiences and traditions in the relationship.

7. Leading with Love

- Base leadership actions on compassion and genuine care.
- Strengthen emotional connections through supportive decisions.
- Support emotional safety and security through empathy.
- Demonstrate patience, kindness, and support consistently.
- Create opportunities to express emotional and physical intimacy.

8. Leading During Crisis

- Take initiative during crises or stressful situations.
- Provide space for open expression of emotions.
- Proactively manage conflicts and threats.
- Commit to protecting the relationship from harmful communication or behaviors.
- Anticipate issues early to support relationship health.
- Support emotional regulation during challenges.
- Ask for and offer support as needed.
- Encourage a team attitude and relationship growth during difficult periods.
- Provide constructive feedback with respect.
- Inspire creative solutions for resolving problems and meeting relationship needs.

We agree to continually work toward building team leadership skills to more effectively meet our needs and guide our relationship in a stable and positive direction. Our leadership goal is to build and maintain a fulfilling and healthy long-term relationship.

RELATIONSHIP TEAM AGREEMENT

We, as partners, acknowledge the significance of teamwork in building and maintaining a healthy relationship. Recognizing that effective teamwork strengthens our bond, improves relationship satisfaction, and reduces overall stress, we agree to uphold the following principles:

1. Mutual Commitment to Teamwork

- Agree to address all relationship problems and needs as a unified team.
- Develop a team attitude that prioritizes relationship needs over individual needs.
- Make decisions and face challenges from a team perspective rather than from an individual view.
- Understand that strong teamwork requires ongoing effort, attention, and sacrifice.
- Balance relationship needs with individual needs.
- Prioritize the health and satisfaction of the relationship as a core commitment.
- Make a commitment to support team agreements and address issues that affect each agreement in a timely and respectful manner.
- Celebrate successful team achievements and offer positive and encouraging feedback.

2. Shared Goals and Vision

- Identify and cultivate a team vision that defines the goals of the relationship.
- Define the specific goals that team attention and energy will be focused on – building intimacy, increasing trust, learning to manage emotions, problem-solving, etc.

- Set a timeline to review team goals and review areas of improvement.
- Make gratitude and appreciation a daily practice to deepen the quality and strength of the relationship.

3. Fair Distribution of Responsibilities

- Define relationship workload and responsibilities, such as chores, finances, parenting, and other responsibilities.
- Determine together who would be best suited for each of the chores and responsibilities.
- Evaluate the level of fairness needed to create a reasonable balance of responsibilities.
- Reach agreement on the overall fairness level moving forward.

4. Effective Communication

- Maintain open, respectful, and honest communication in all aspects of the relationship.
- Create a safe space to express needs, concerns, and opinions without fear of judgment, criticism, or negativity.
- Communicate about relationship needs, and highlight which ones need particular attention.
- Encourage complete openness about specific needs and desires.
- Regularly express appreciation for how each partner contributes to the team.

5. Emotional and Social Needs

- Evaluate activities that provide mutual pleasure.
- Create a pleasure menu of enjoyable activities that build relationship quality.
- Determine social needs and how to share them together.

- Prioritize shared social relationships over other personal relationships.
- Validate and support each other's emotional experiences
- Work together to regulate emotional stress and support each other during difficult times.
- Celebrate each other's accomplishments—big or small—as shared wins.
- Acknowledge and appreciate when team efforts lead to growth or success.

6. Financial Needs

- Evaluate financial resources and needs.
- Create a budget to determine financial income and expenses.
- Collaborate on budgeting, saving, spending, and setting financial goals.
- Identify where expenses can be reduced without sacrificing quality of life.
- Determine how extra money would best be spent – savings, home needs, vacations, etc.

7. Time Management

- Create a time budget that allows for adequate time to meet both individual and team needs.
- Determine the best times for completing specific chores and responsibilities.
- Determine the ideal times for sharing physical intimacy.
- Factor in time needed for other social relationships – family, friends, etc.
- Build in time for pleasure and fun.
- Encourage time spent on relationship education (books, counseling, workshops, etc.).

- Set aside regular, dedicated time to discuss relationship needs, goals, and concerns.

8. Team Approach to Problem-Solving and Decision-Making

- Identify the best time and place to discuss relationships issues and needs.
- Determine a backup time if the regular time needs to be changed.
- Avoid busy or challenging times when distractions, fatigue, or emotional stress can interfere with effective problem-solving.
- Develop effective ways to complete chores and responsibilities in a more efficient way.
- Approach problems and conflicts with a supportive team mindset.
- Maintain a positive and collaborative team attitude that strengthens the relationship.
- Seek intelligent and creative solutions to problems and responsibilities through respectful dialogue and compromise.
- Reduce stress and promote relationship stability by resolving conflicts collaboratively.
- Recognize that relationship needs and circumstances may change over time.
- Plan to review and adjust team agreements to reflect changing needs.
- Remain flexible and supportive in responding to life transitions or evolving needs.
- Remember that generosity and sacrifice are essential to teamwork.
- Use a shared decision-making approach for choices that affect both partners.
- Value each other's ideas and perspective in making decisions.

- Strive to make decisions that reflect mutual interests and needs.
- Make team decisions that maximize the care and growth of the relationship.
- Avoid power struggles by prioritizing collaboration over control.

9. Crisis and Stress Management

- Be emotionally present, dependable, and responsive during difficult times – such as illness, grief, or job loss.
- Adjust responsibilities when one partner is emotionally or physically overloaded.
- Approach stressful situations and challenges as opportunities to strengthen resilience and deepen emotional connection.
- Take responsibility for how communication and emotional regulation shape the relationship environment during stressful times.
- Maintain support for each other through the process of managing conflict.
- When emotionally overwhelmed, agree to disengage before communication and behaviors become toxic or unhealthy for the relationship.
- After a crisis or emotionally difficult interaction, set time aside to talk about what worked, what did not, and how to improve the process for the future.

By adhering to these teamwork principles, we commit ourselves to building a resilient, supportive, efficient, and deeply satisfying partnership - one that endures and flourishes through all of life's challenges.

HONESTY AGREEMENT

We, as partners, mutually agree to maintain honesty as a core principle within our relationship, recognizing its importance for trust, security, and emotional intimacy. Therefore, we commit ourselves to the following:

1. Commitment to Honesty

- Communicate truthfully, directly, and transparently in all interactions.
- Share thoughts, feelings, and needs in a sincere and genuine way.
- Strive to speak based on an accurate understanding rather than one based on assumptions.
- Maintain honesty in daily interactions and align words with actions to build consistent trust.
- Practice integrity in what you do and how you do it.

2. Honesty as the Foundation for Trust and Security

- Communicate truthfully, directly, and transparently in all interactions.
- Share accurate and truthful information, even when it's difficult or uncomfortable.
- Provide a consistent environment of honesty to create emotional safety.
- Uphold truthfulness as a pillar for building and maintaining trust.
- Encourage open expression of beliefs and emotions without fear of judgment.
- Respond to honesty with support and understanding to encourage openness.

3. Emotional Intimacy Through Honest Communication

- Respond to honesty with support and understanding to encourage openness.
- Be open in sharing vulnerable emotions, desires, and experiences.
- Invite closeness by expressing your genuine thoughts and feelings.
- Treat honesty as a pathway to deeper emotional connection and intimacy.
- Initiate open conversations around sensitive or emotionally charged topics.

4. Compassionate and Respectful Honesty

- Deliver difficult truths with care, compassion, and emotional responsibility.
- Avoid using honesty as a weapon to criticize, shame, or hurt.
- Always preserve your partner's dignity in moments of vulnerability.
- Avoid expressing emotionally charged information without preparation or sensitivity.
- Consider timing and your partner's emotional readiness when sharing difficult truths.

5. Honesty in Conflict and Repair

- Approach disagreements directly and openly rather than become evasive or defensive.
- Take responsibility for statements that were wrong, distorted, over-exaggerated, or dishonest.
- Avoid distortion of facts or minimizing issues because they are uncomfortable to talk about.

6. Self-Awareness and Personal Responsibility

- Take time to be honest with yourself before speaking with your partner.
- Recognize when personal biases, insecurities, or assumptions shape your truth.
- Acknowledge that misunderstandings often arise in emotionally charged situations.
- Avoid deliberately withholding or omitting the truth.

7. Honesty and Respect for Privacy

- Normalize regular check-ins about where each partner stands on an issue of concern.
- Balance transparency with respect for personal boundaries and privacy.
- Clarify what privacy means for each partner and distinguish it from secrecy.

By honoring these principles of honesty, we commit ourselves to a relationship strengthened by trust, genuineness, and shared emotional intimacy. This ongoing commitment ensures the health, stability, and emotional satisfaction of our long-term partnership.

FAIRNESS AGREEMENT

We, as partners, mutually agree that fairness is an essential part of the foundation of a stable and balanced relationship. Recognizing that fairness significantly contributes to relationship stability, emotional closeness, and satisfaction, we agree to commit ourselves to the following:

1. Commitment to Fairness

- Be open about what we feel is fair and unfair in our relationship.
- Through mutual commitment make fairness a priority in our relationship.
- Strive to maintain fairness across all levels.
- Express gratitude for your partner's efforts at striving for fairness.
- Strive for clarity in terms of what is needed for there to be fairness in the relationship.
- View fairness and sacrifice as an expression of deep, genuine care for each other.
- Accept that a perfect level of fairness is sometimes not achievable.
- Use fairness in deciding how time, energy, and focus are applied to relationship needs and personal needs.

2. Reciprocity and Generosity

- Use the principle of reciprocity as a guiding principle in the relationship.
- Give generously when asked for help.
- Focus more on giving to the relationship than on getting from the relationship.

3. Communication

- Work together to find fair and equitable solutions when differences arise.
- Express gratitude for efforts made by each partner to compromise.
- Regularly discuss responsibilities to ensure a balance of chores and tasks.

4. Shared Responsibilities

- Identify the needs and obligations of the relationship.
- Distribute responsibilities fairly, based on individual strengths and capacities.
- Divide household chores, finances, child-rearing, cooking, cleaning, shopping, and other responsibilities in an equitable manner.
- Make space for each person's autonomy and self-care, while also investing in shared responsibilities and experiences.

5. Acceptance and Caring

- Balance responsibilities to compensate for imbalances that may arise in other areas.
- Accept each other's strengths and limitations with understanding and compassion.
- Express care and appreciation for what each partner contributes to the relationship.

6. Financial Transparency

- Maintain financial openness and transparency.
- Express financial needs clearly to avoid problems with non-disclosure.

- Commit to open conversations about financial expectations, goals, and contributions.
- Ensure that we both feel empowered and respected in financial decision-making.

7. Fairness in Decision-Making

- Ensure that both voices are heard and valued when making major decisions.
- Avoid making unilateral decisions that impact both partners without mutual consent.
- Avoid keeping score in terms of who is getting the most from the relationship.
- Learn to determine when and where sacrifice is necessary for the health and quality of the relationship.

8. Remedies for Unfairness

- Address and remedy imbalances if one partner becomes unfairly burdened
- Commit to resolving issues of fairness before they lead to chronic stress or resentment.
- Engage in regular, constructive conversations to maintain or restore fairness and equity.

9. Fairness in Conflict Recovery

- Share the emotional work involved when initiating reconnection after conflicts.
- Avoid placing responsibility for emotional repair on only one partner.
- Share goals of forgiveness, healing, and reconnection.

We pledge to honor these principles of fairness and will continuously strive to seek a balanced and equitable distribution of responsibilities as we move forward to meet life's challenges. We agree to honor and respect each other's efforts at being generous with time, energy, and the intention to maintain a fair and satisfying long-term relationship.

INTIMACY AND NURTURANCE AGREEMENT

We, as partners, mutually acknowledge and agree that our love and intimacy are cherished gifts that forms the foundation of a successful, lasting relationship. We recognize that love, intimacy, and nurturance are essential for long-term health, stability, and emotional fulfillment in our partnership. Love is not merely a feeling, but a dynamic, evolving experience sustained through ongoing care, emotional engagement, and mutual understanding. With that understanding, we commit to the following:

1. Commitment to Love and Nurturance

- Commit to nurturing a relationship rooted in emotional fulfillment, love, and mutual care.
- Express love intentionally through words, gestures, and physical closeness.
- Prioritize regular moments of connection and tenderness.
- Recognize nurturance as the emotional lifeline of the relationship.
- Invest time, energy, and attention in meeting each other's unique emotional and physical needs.

2. Communication and Emotional Expression

- Express words of love, appreciation, and reassurance often.
- Share needs and desires openly and without fear of judgment.
- Create space for honest conversations about emotional and sexual intimacy.
- Listen with focused attention using empathy, patience, and presence.

3. Physical and Sexual Intimacy

- Celebrate physical intimacy as a vital expression of love and connection.
- Engage in affectionate touch—holding hands, hugging, cuddling, and gentle presence.
- Share desires, boundaries, and needs with honesty and care.
- Prioritize time and space for intimacy that feels emotionally safe, mutually respectful, and joyfully shared.

4. Nurturing Behaviors and Daily Acts of Care

- Show love through thoughtful daily acts—kindness, helpfulness, encouragement.
- Offer nurturing through words, touch, and intentional gestures.
- Stay attuned to your partner's unique ways of feeling loved and respond with care.
- Let your love be visible, consistent, and heartfelt in everyday actions.

5. Mutual Understanding and Changing Needs

- Recognize that emotional and physical needs evolve over time.
- Approach changes with curiosity, flexibility, and compassion.
- Regularly "check-in" to understand and adapt to each other's needs.
- Explore preferences for intimacy regarding its expression, frequency, and emotional tone.

6. Emotional Safety and Responsiveness

- Create an environment where vulnerability is met with warmth and respect.

- Be emotionally available and responsive to your partner's signals for connection.
- Recognize and honor subtle expressions of desire - a look, a sigh, a touch.
- Let empathy, sensitivity, and trust guide your responses in emotionally charged moments.

7. Quality Time and Being Present

- When together, be fully present - emotionally, mentally, and physically.
- Protect your shared time from distractions and interruptions.
- Create shared patterns of intimate engagement through daily check-ins, bedtime routines, or during free time together.

8. Healing Disconnection and Rekindling Closeness

- Acknowledge that emotional or physical disconnection can happen in any relationship.
- Approach moments of distance as opportunities for repair and reconnection.
- Identify pathways that restore closeness and emotional safety.
- Use healing and reconnection to strengthen intimacy and deepen understanding.

9. Growth and Intimacy

- Allow your intimacy to evolve—through exploration, openness, and creativity.
- Invite playfulness, flirtation, and lightheartedness into your connection.

- Treat your relationship as a journey of mutual discovery and growing pleasure.
- Embrace shared growth as a source of deepened love and renewed connection.

10. Appreciation and Gratitude

- Notice and celebrate the ways your partner expresses love and care.
- Offer gratitude for effort, vulnerability, and thoughtful gestures.
- Reinforce connection through praise, appreciation, and heartfelt affirmations.
- Treat even the smallest moments as meaningful opportunities for love and nurturance.

Through adherence to these principles, we commit ourselves to supporting and nurturing our love for each other. Through our expressions of love and nurturance, we will strive to build and sustain a healthy and emotionally fulfilling lifelong partnership.

RELATIONSHIP SECURITY AGREEMENT

We, as partners, acknowledge and affirm that safety and security are a critical part of the foundation of our relationship. We recognize that safety and security are necessary to maintain trust, emotional stability, and enduring intimacy. Therefore, we mutually agree to uphold the following principles:

1. Mutual Commitment to Security

- Always prioritize each other's feelings of safety and security.
- Acknowledge safety and security as essential for a thriving, long-term relationship.
- Consistently work to create an environment free from harm, threat, and insecurity.
- Address all issues of insecurity in a timely and open manner.

2. Physical Security

- Commit to physical safety as a non-negotiable foundation of our partnership.
- Maintain zero tolerance for violence, abuse, or threats of physical harm.
- Actively cultivate a physically safe and secure environment.

3. Security in Sexual Intimacy

- Reaffirm the importance of consent, comfort, and mutual satisfaction regarding physical intimacy.
- Create a safe environment in which to express specific desires and needs regarding affection and sexual intimacy.

- Encourage the exploration of physical intimacy in ways that deepen engagement.
- Understand that sexual needs and preferences may change over time and may require adaptation, sacrifice, and adjustments.
- Address any area of physical intimacy that causes discomfort or concern in an open and direct manner without pressure or judgment.

4. Emotional Security

- Offer consistent emotional support, respect, and reassurance.
- Care for each other's feelings, needs, and insecurities with emotional support.
- Build and maintain trust by discussing insecurities openly and compassionately.

5. Security in Social Situations

- Prioritize our relationship over other relationships that disrupt the ability to maintain a healthy balance and reinforce emotional security.
- Openly discuss concerns about outside relationships respectfully.
- Maintain healthy boundaries in all social relationships regarding time and commitment.

6. Financial Security

- Communicate openly and honestly about all financial matters.
- Manage financial resources equitably and cooperatively.
- Address financial decisions as a team to help prevent

individual decisions causing financial and emotional insecurity.

7. Respect for Independence

- Acknowledge and support each other's need for personal space and independence.
- Encourage individual growth by respecting personal interests and activities.
- Seek to reinforce healthy independence so that it strengthens rather than threatens relationship security.

8. Strategies for Building a Secure Relationship

- Speak openly, honestly, and respectfully about any source of insecurity or concern.
- Actively listen, show empathy, and respond constructively to manage emotional distress.
- Address misunderstandings early to maintain a secure connection.
- Respond with compassion whenever concerns or insecurities are expressed.
- Create time and space for sharing fears, insecurities, or sensitive emotions without fear of judgment or dismissal.
- Honor vulnerability as a strength and respond with compassion and presence.
- Commit to an ongoing effort and dialogue to preserve the security needed for an emotionally fulfilling partnership.
- Disclose relevant outside contact or interactions transparently to avoid misunderstandings.
- Create shared plans to build a sense of predictability and commitment.
- Revisit goals and vision regularly to maintain a mutual sense of direction.

- Provide reassurance and emotional support during times of major life change - job loss, illness, grief, etc.
- Regularly affirm your love, commitment, and appreciation.
- Express gratitude for each other's presence and contributions to the relationship.

9. Preventing Insecurities

- Identify and discuss potential sources of insecurity before they become larger issues.
- Recognize and have open dialogue to resolve or minimize security threats.
- Be proactive in protecting the emotional well-being of each partner.
- Avoid using shared vulnerabilities against each other.

10. Recovering from Security Breaches

- Recognize that issues can occur that lead to emotional insecurity – violations of trust, harsh words, dishonesty, neglect, etc.
- Use reassurance as a tool to rebuild security during periods of stress or uncertainty.
- Commit to repairing security with support and accountability in a timely manner.
- Rebuild security and trust through transparency, consistent reassurance, and genuine change.
- Seek professional guidance or outside support for security concerns that cannot be resolved.
- Regularly revisit and update shared security needs and commitments.

Through these commitments, we pledge to make every effort to support the need for security in our relationship. We agree to cultivate a relationship characterized by mutual trust, emotional stability, and a deep level of security to ensure that we are able to maintain a healthy and stable long-term relationship.

RELATIONSHIP PROBLEM-SOLVING AGREEMENT

We recognize that effective problem-solving is an essential need in building and maintaining a healthy, intimate relationship. The strength, quality, and durability of our relationship depends on how well we work together as a team in working out the problems and challenges that we will face together. To support this essential need, we commit to the following principles:

1. Problem-Solving Approach

- Acknowledge that all couples experience problems and conflicts and that addressing and resolving problems is essential for the long-term health and stability of our relationship.
- Be aware that the approach taken to solve problems is often more important than the problem itself.
- Adopt a team-oriented and solution-focused mindset.
- Commit to resolving problems with teamwork, cooperation and patience.
- Approach all issues with a shared goal of mutual understanding, need fulfillment, and relationship health.

2. Emotions and Conflict in Problem-Solving

- Be aware that emotional reactions to problems can be more harmful than the problems themselves.
- Regulate and manage anger, frustration, and anxiety to prevent them from causing damage to the relationship.
- Provide help and support when emotionally distressed.
- During periods of conflict, use the "Rule of 10" where each partner rates how important the issue is using a 1–10 scale, with 10 being the highest level of importance.

- Maintain control over negative emotions that lead to toxic communication.

3. Communication Skills for Problem-solving

- Commit to effective, clear, and respectful communication during problem-solving.
- Use questions to gain clarity and avoid assumptions or misinterpretations.
- Confirm mutual understanding before moving to solutions.
- Pause before responding during conflict.
- Listen first, in order to understand better.
- Prioritize facts over assumptions, and agreement over conflict.
- Use supportive questions to gain clarity and avoid emotional overload.

4. Structured Approach to Managing Problems

- Establish predictable times and spaces for discussing issues.
- Recognize that complex issues may require multiple conversations.
- Address problems in a timely manner.
- Maintain a positive focus throughout discussions.
- Focus on one problem at a time
- Focus on facts, not only feelings.

5. Identify the Underlying Need of the Problem

- Clearly define the problem, including when, how often, and how it affects each partner.
- Explore three perspectives: your own, your partner's, and the relationship team perspective.

- Identify the underlying needs that the problem represents.
- Understand that most solutions are not perfect and may require compromise and sacrifice.
- Give solutions time to work effectively.

6. Problem-Solving Steps

- Clearly define and describe the problem.
- Manage emotional reactions throughout the discussion.
- Identify the core needs underlying the issue.
- Brainstorm and evaluate potential solutions.
- Agree on the best possible solution collaboratively.
- Implement the chosen solution as a team.
- Evaluate whether the solution is working effectively.
- Make improvements or adjustments as necessary.
- Draw confidence and clarity from strategies that worked in the past.
- Maintain a team-oriented approach to problem-solving.

7. Teamwork

- Brainstorm multiple solutions that might address the issue.
- Discuss pros and cons of potential strategies.
- Collaborate to select the best solutions that meet the needs of both partners.
- Approach all problems as a shared issue, not one person's fault or burden.
- Frame problems with collective language: "How can we work through this?"
- Acknowledge prior successes in resolving issues together.

8. Avoiding Common Pitfalls in Problem-Solving

- Avoid aggressive, oppositional, or emotionally reactive communication and behaviors.
- Avoid trying to address problems during periods of high stress or inappropriate times – such as late at night, when already upset, while at work, etc.
- Resist the urge to bring up old or past issues during current discussions.
- Avoid being dismissive or defensive.

9. Problem-Solving Recovery

- Follow-up to determine what worked well and what could be improved next time.
- Develop rituals for emotional reconnection after challenging conversations – shifting to more positive topics, going for a walk, hugging, or sharing some enjoyable activity.
- View your partner's struggle as a signal of unmet needs, not a personal flaw.
- Replace blame with curiosity and empathy.
- Normalize repair as part of a healthy relationship.
- Return to unresolved issues with openness and a renewed desire to address issues.
- Agree to seek professional help if a problem becomes chronic or unresolvable.

We agree to prioritize and continuously improve our ability to resolve problems in a cooperative and supportive team-oriented manner. This agreement will allow us to maintain a healthy and satisfying relationship that can endure the everyday problems and challenges that we must face.

STRESS MANAGEMENT AGREEMENT

We, as partners, mutually agree that emotional stress and conflict are an inevitable part of every relationship. We understand that how we manage emotional reactions plays a vital role in the health, longevity, and emotional satisfaction of our relationship. For these reasons, we commit to the following principles:

1. Commitment to Managing Stress

- We recognize that the ability to manage emotional stress is essential to maintaining a high-quality, healthy relationship.
- We will lead our relationship with calm, patience and compassion, especially during emotionally stressful interactions.
- Protect our relationship and reinforce trust, care, and mutual respect.
- Practice emotional leadership and encourage a pattern of positive emotional expression.
- Lead with love, rather than be led by negative emotional reactions.

2. Respect for Relationship Health

- Recognize that emotional expression plays a major role in the long-term health of the relationship.
- Take responsibility for protecting and replenishing the emotional health of our connection.
- Express communication and behaviors that supports and reinforces security, nurturance, and the long-term wellbeing of our relationship.

3. Personal Responsibility for Emotional Reactions

- Accept full responsibility for one's emotional responses.
- Develop personal tools and strategies to regulate strong emotions - positive thinking, calming imagery, breathing techniques.
- Commit to using positive thinking to manage emotional reactions.

4. Supportive Communication and Compassionate Listening

- Listen attentively when one's partner is expressing emotional stress.
- Avoid interruptions to encourage the full expression of thought and emotions.
- Speak calmly and use supportive language to facilitate a sense of security and safety.
- Reduce emotional intensity by slowing down the rate of speech and softening the volume.

5. Building Emotional Management Skills

- Regularly practice emotional regulation tools such as:
- Positive self-calming thoughts
- Deep breathing
- Progressive muscle relaxation
- Calming imagery and success visualization
- Commit to learning and reinforcing new tools even when not in conflict, so they are
- View emotional self-regulation as a form of love and leadership in the relationship.

6. Team Approach to Conflict and Stress

- Treat conflict and emotional stress as shared challenges to overcome together as a team.

- Align as partners, not opponents, when addressing stressful issues and problems.
- Support each other in the de-escalation of overwhelming emotionally stress.
- Commit to team strategies for managing emotionally harmful communication.

7. Identify Emotional Triggers

- Identify and respect each other's known emotional triggers.
- Determine when, where, and what situations or events lead to strong emotional reactions.
- Evaluate the frequency of significant emotional reactions that place stress on the relationship.
- Commit to pausing and calming down before reacting to emotional triggers.

8. Navigating Conflict

- Learn to recognize communication patterns that lead to conflict, hostility, or withdrawal.
- Avoid the factors that escalate emotional reactions – raising one's voice, negative or hostile responses, rolling one's eyes, etc.
- Practice self-calming and emotional regulation to prevent and interrupt harmful communication.
- Prioritize respect and emotional safety during periods of escalating emotional reactions.
- View an emotional reaction as a form of personal distress that reflects a need.
- Provide support when emotions are expressed, in order to strengthen connection.

9. Avoidance of Harmful Communication

- Consciously avoid communication or behavior that is hurtful, disrespectful, or abusive.
- Refrain from inflammatory language - sarcasm, blame, contempt, and hostility.
- Protect the security and safety of the relationship to ensure relationship health.
- Avoid placing blame for emotionally negative communication on one's partner.
- When necessary, use disengagement as a temporary strategy to protect the relationship.
- Do not use disengagement as a form of punishment, avoidance, or rejection.
- Recognize the early signs of harmful communication and behaviors before the need for disengagement becomes necessary.
- Communicate the intent to disengage with care, and to re-engage when in a more emotionally calm state.

10. Recovery from Emotionally Stressful Conflicts

- Show that emotional repair is a shared responsibility, requiring both partners to listen, take responsibility, and offer forgiveness.
- Create a safe space for problem-solving discussions.
- Take emotional breaks when needed but return to the discussion with the intention to resolve the issue in a supportive and cooperative manner.
- Use cooperative language that focuses on shared goals and solutions.
- Revisit challenging conversations after calming down, approaching them with openness, accountability, and empathy.
- Respond with respect when one partner seeks to re-engage after disengagement.

- Seek professional guidance and support when unable to find successful strategies for managing emotional reactions that lead to harmful communication or behaviors.

We agree to prioritize and continuously improve our ability to manage relationship stress in a cooperative and supportive manner. The purpose of this agreement is to allow us to maintain a healthy and satisfying long-term relationship by effectively managing stress and protecting our relationship from harm caused by negative emotional reactions.

NOTES

Chapman, Gary. *The 5 Languages of Love: The Secret to Love That Lasts.* Northfield Publishing, (2015).

Cloud, Henry. *Trust: Knowing When to Give It, When to Withhold It, How to Earn It, and How to Fix It When It Gets Broken.* Worthy books, (2023).

Comfort, A. *The Joy of Sex: The Ultimate Revised Edition.* New York: Crown Publishing Group, (2009).

Feldhahn, S. *The Surprising Secrets of Highly Happy Marriages: The Little Things That Make a Big Difference.* Multnomah Books, (2013).

Fletcher, G. J. O., Simpson, J. A., Campbell, L., & Overall, N.C. *The Science of Intimate Relationships.* Wiley-Blackwell, (2013).

Gottman, John, Ph.D., Gottman, Julie Swartz, Ph.D., Abrams, Doug, and Carlton Abrams, Rachel, M.D. *Eight Dates: Essential Conversations for a Lifetime of Love.* Workman Publishing Company. (February 5, 2019).

Gottman, John, Ph.D., and Silver, Nan. What Makes Love Last? *How To Build Trust and Avoid Betrayal.* Simon & Schuster, (2012).

Gottman, John, Ph.D., and Silver, Nan. *The Seven Principles for Making Marriage Work.* Harmony Books, May 5, 2015. (Original publication - 1999).

Greenberg, M. *The Stress-Proof Brain: Master Your Emotional Response to Stress Using Mindfulness and Neuroplasticity.* New Harbinger, (2017).

Hendrix, Harville, Ph.D. and Hunt, Helen Ph.D. *Getting the Love You Want: A Guide for Couples.* Saint Martin's Griffin, New York. (2019 Reprint).

Joannides, P. *The Guide to Getting It On.* Goofy Foot Press. (2021).

Johnson, Sue. *Hold Me Tight: Seven Conversations for a Lifetime of Love.* Little, Brown, and Company. (April 8, 2008).

Johnson, Sue. *Love Sense: The Revolutionary New Science of Romantic Relationships.* Little, Brown Spark (2013).

Le, B.M., Chee, P., Shimshock, C.J., & Le, J. *Expressed and Perceived Honesty Benefits Relationships Even When Couples Are Not Accurate.* Social Psychological and Personality Science (2025).

Levine, Amir; and Heller, Rachel. *Attached: The New Science of Adult Attachment and How It Can Help You Find and Keep Love.* Tarcher-Perigee. (2011).

Markman, H.J., Stanley, S.M., Rhoades, G.K., & Levine, J.R. *Fighting for Your Marriage: Positive Steps for Preventing Divorce and Building a Lasting Love.* (4th edition). Jossey-Bass/ Wiley, (2024).

Maslow, A.H., *A Theory of Motivation.* Martino Find Books, (June 11, 2013).

Nagoski, E., *Come as You Are: The Surprising New Science That Will Transform Your Sex Life.* (2015).

Perel, Esther. *Mating in Captivity: Unlocking Erotic Intelligence.* Harper Collins. (Oct. 2017).

Real, Terrence. *The New Rules of Marriage: What You Need to Know to Make Love Work.* Ballantine Books. (2007).

Real, Terrence. *Us: Getting Past You & Me to Build a More Loving Relationship.* Unabridged edition. Goop Press / Random House Audio. (2022).

Rodsky, Eve. *Fair Play: A Game Changing Solution for When You Have Too Much to Do (and More Life to Live).* G.P. Putnam's Sons (2019).

Rosenberg, Marshall B., *Nonviolent Communication: A Language of Life.* PuddleDancer Press. (3rd edition, 2015).

Ryan, Richard M., and Deci, Edward L. *Self-Determination Theory: Basic Psychological Needs in Motivation, Development, and Wellness.* The Guilford Press. (Nov. 2018).

Sloan, Alfred P. Foundation. *The Ecology of Working Families: The Sloan Study of Working Families.* New York, NY: Alfred P. Sloan Foundation. (2001).

Sofer, Jay Oren. *Say What You Mean: A Mindful Approach to Nonviolent Communication.* Shambhala Publications. (Dec. 11, 2018).

Sternberg, R.J. & Barnes, M.L. *The Psychology of Love.* Yale University Press., (1988).

YouGov Survey of Relationship Values. (Jan. 2025).

Young, G., Zeigler-Hill, V. *The Dual-Pathway Model of Respect in Romantic Relationships.* Sexes, 2024, 5, 317-334.

ACKNOWLEDGMENTS

To the many teachers and clients who have shaped my understanding and deepened my insight—thank you for the lessons, the trust, and the inspiration.

To all those within and beyond my family with whom I've shared the journey of Relationship Wealth, your stories and presence have made this work truly meaningful.

A special acknowledgment to Victoria, whose relentless support helped to make the completion of this book possible.

And finally, to anyone who has ever struggled in love or longed for something more—may this book serve as your guide and help you build a lifetime of Relationship Wealth.

www.ingramcontent.com/pod-product-compliance
Lightning Source LLC
Chambersburg PA
CBHW031119020426